D1509481

Grill It!

Grill It!
Seafood

**80 Quick and Delicious Recipes
to Sear, Sizzle, and Smoke**

Edited by Anne McDowall

AN IMPRINT OF RUNNING PRESS
PHILADELPHIA · LONDON

2003 Salamander Books Ltd
Published by Salamander Books Ltd.
8 Blenheim Court, Brewery Road
London N7 9NY, United Kingdom

© Salamander Books Ltd. 2003
A member of **Chrysalis** Books plc

This edition published in the United States in 2003 by Courage Books, an imprint of
Running Press Book Publishers

All rights reserved under the Pan-American and International Copyright Conventions.

This book may not be reproduced in whole or in part, in any form or by any means, electronic or
mechanical, including photocopying, recording, or by any information storage and retrieval system now
known or hereafter invented, without written permission from the publisher.

1 3 5 7 9 8 6 4 2

Library of Congress Cataloging-in-Publication Number 2002108138

ISBN 0-7624-1492-8

Notice: The information contained in this book is true and complete to the best of our knowledge. All
recommendations are made without any guarantee on the part of the author or publisher. The author and
publisher disclaim all liability in connection with the use of this information.

Credits

Editor: Anne McDowall
Project Manager: Katherine Edelston
Designer: Cara Hamilton
Production: Ian Hughes
Color reproduction: Anorax Imaging Ltd.
Printed in China

The recipes in this book have appeared in previous Salamander titles by other authors and have been edited
by Anne McDowall for this edition.

Notes

All spoon measurements are level: 1 teaspoon = 5ml spoon; 1 tablespoon = 15ml spoon
Cooking times given are approximate: they will vary according to the starting temperature of the food and
its thickness as well as the heat of the grill.
All recipes in this book assume that fish has been cleaned and scaled.

Contents

Introduction

What better way to cook all sorts of fish than on a grill—it's quick, it's healthy, and the fish not only retains all its natural flavor, but can also be enhanced by wonderfully exotic spices in marinades, glazes, and accompanying dips and sauces. As with any grilling, there are a few things you need to know—for food to taste its best and to be safe—but barbecues are basically fun, social occasions, so relax and experiment!

Choosing a grill

There is a variety of different types of grill available, so if you are just starting out, or want to replace your existing model, it's worth taking some time to think about the various options to help you decide which would suit you best.

Although the traditional grill burns charcoal (or wood), there's a lot to be said for a gas or electric alternative. Neither requires starter fuel and both retain heat evenly. Gas grills, in particular, ignite almost instantaneously (electric types take about 10 minutes to heat) and can be used at any time of year. Their main disadvantage is the cumbersome gas bottle, which all models require. Although, of course, electric grills must not be used in the rain, the more sophisticated models can be used indoors with suitable ducting.

Purists argue that the fun of grilling is cooking over a real fire. Another big advantage of charcoal-burning models is their cost: a basic model will be cheaper than its gas or electric counterpart. Although you have the ongoing cost of fuel, neither lumpwood

Grill accessories

As well as the grill, suitable fuel and firelighters, there are a number of other tools and accessories that are worth considering. Some are virtually indispensable; others will be very useful for cooking particular foods.

- Wooden block or table—for keeping implements and tools close at hand.
- Wire baskets—rectangular hinged meshes and fish-shaped ones are ideal for holding delicate fish that are being cooked directly on the grill and enable them to be turned easily.
- Skewers—square metal, long wooden, or bamboo. The latter need to be soaked for about 20 minutes before use.
- Tongs and forks—ones with long handles are essential to keep hands away from heat source.
- Metal griddle plate—for cooking certain fragile foods on.
- Brushes—for basting food while it is cooking.
- Heavy-duty aluminum foil—for wrapping food to be cooked on the grill.
- Battery-operated fan—useful for fanning coals.
- Apron—a thick one with pockets is ideal.
- Oven gloves—but avoid the double-handed types.
- Water sprayer—for dousing unruly flames.
- Stiff wire brush and metal scrapers—for cleaning the grill.

charcoal nor pressed briquettes (the most popular fuel types) are very expensive. Of the two, the former is the cheaper, lights more easily, and burns hotter, but pressed briquettes burn longer once alight. It is also possible to buy aromatic wood chips to place on the ashen coals, which will impart wonderful, subtle flavors to the food.

Assuming you don't choose a disposable grill—basically a tin tray containing charcoal—the simplest option is a shallow metal bowl on a frame. There is no venting or cover but it is easy to light and simple to control. Better still is a kettle grill with its own hood, which will be suitable for all types of cooking—the hood will help protect food in bad weather, prevent spattering and billowing of smoke, and will also enable you to smoke food.

Always choose a larger model than you think you might need—even if you only cook small amounts of food, this will allow you to move the food around, to hotter or cooler areas as necessary.

Safety checklist
- Position the grill carefully on even ground and away from trees and fences.
- Never use gasoline, denatured alcohol, or paraffin to light a grill.
- Avoid using an electric grill in wet weather.
- Never leave a lit grill unattended and be particularly vigilant with children.
- Keep a water spray handy to douse flames if they become unruly.
- Use long-handled tools to keep hands away from flames and avoid double-handed oven gloves, which can easily catch in the flames.
- Allow a transportable grill to cool completely before packing it away.
- Hot embers take several hours to cool: make sure they are cold before disposing of them.

Cooking on the grill
Before you light the grill, ensure it is in the right position, as a lit grill will be heavy—and possibly unsafe—to move. Spread a single layer of coals over the base, pile them up a little in the center, and push in firelighters or jelly starters. (Follow the manufacturer's instructions carefully if you are using ignition fluid and never use gasoline, denatured alcohol, paraffin, or other similar flammable liquids.) Light with a taper and, as soon as the fire has caught, spread out coals and add a few more. The grill is ready to start cooking on only when the flames have died down and the charcoal is covered with white ash—this will usually take at least half an hour. Charcoal will burn about an hour and a half and you can add other pieces around the edges occasionally.

Although it is easy to adjust the heat on gas and electric grills, it is more difficult on an open-grid type unless you have a kettle grill with adjustable vents. If the coals have become too hot, either place the food away from the center of the grill or push coals aside to distribute their heat. To make the fire hotter, poke away the ash, push coals together, and gently blow (or use a battery-operated fan). To test the temperature of the grill, place your open hand carefully over the coals: if you can keep it there as long as 5 seconds, the temperature is low; 3 or 4 seconds it is medium-hot, and 2 seconds it is hot. The right height for cooking is about 2 to 3 inches above the grid. On a lidded grill, the heat will be greater when the lid is lowered.

When you have finished cooking, spread out the coals so that they cool faster. Cleaning the grill rack is best done while still hot: use a metal scraper to dislodge bits of food into the fire. If necessary, you can wash the grill rack with soapy water once it has cooled. When the embers are completely cold (this will take several hours), sift away surplus ash and cover the grill for future use.

Choosing fish

Really fresh fish looks bright with vivid markings. The eyes are clear, bright, and slightly protruding and the gills pinkish or bright red (brown gills are a sure sign fish is stale). Skin is firm and bright with bright scales that adhere tightly. The flesh is firm and elastic and springs back when pressed. Any smell is fresh and clean with a hint of the sea (exceptions are shark and skate, which give off a natural smell of ammonia, which disappears on cooking).

Fillets and steaks should feel firm, the cut surfaces look translucent rather than opaque, and they should not be dry or shrivelled. Avoid any that look slimy or have brown or yellow patches at the edges. If packaged, there should not be any milky liquid.

A lot of the fish sold in supermarkets, and some fish markets, is thawed frozen fish. This has an unfortunate toll on its quality and limits its life. Thawed frozen fish should not be refrozen.

Substitutions

As fish and seafood are regional and seasonal, you may not be able to buy the type specified in a recipe, but substitutions are often possible, especially for fillets or steaks. Below are some examples:
Sole / brill / flounder
Brill / turbot / John Dory
Porgy / scup / red bream
Cod / haddock / halibut / hake / monkfish
Red snapper / grouper / mahi mahi (dolphin fish)
Pompano / pomfret / red snapper
Tuna / swordfish
Mackerel / herring
Bass / salmon (especially steaks and fillets)

Preparing and cooking fish

The recipes in this book assume that fish has been cleaned and scaled; a fishmonger will do this for you. Skinning round fish presents no problems, but skinning flat fish, such as flounder, is more difficult and you may prefer to get your fishmonger to do it for you. Filleting is quick and easy after a little practice and providing you use a filleting knife. This has a flexible, pointed, straight-edged blade about 6 inches long. With this type of knife you can feel round soft fish bones, removing every last scrap of flesh from them. A really sharp edge to the blade is vital for skinning, boning, or filleting fish quickly, easily, and efficiently. However, fish skin will blunt the edge of the knife quickly, so it will need frequent sharpening. You will also need a heavy knife for removing fish heads, kitchen scissors for snipping away fins, a large board, and a clean damp cloth. Handle skinned and filleted fish with care and cook as soon as possible. Keep trimmings for stock.

Using marinades Marinades are often used with foods that are to be grilled: not only does oil in a marinade help prevent food from sticking, but added herbs and spices create mouthwatering flavors. Fish and shellfish generally require a shorter marinating time than meat. If food has been marinated in the refrigerator, allow it to come back to room temperature before cooking.

Grilling Many types of fish are suitable for cooking directly on top of the flame, but delicate varieties are best contained in a hinged wire basket.

Cooking in foil Delicate fish can also be wrapped in heavy-duty or double-thickness aluminum foil. Wrapping fish also helps to prevent the outside of the food from burning before the inside is cooked and keeps juices trapped inside.

Pan-frying You can use a griddle or heavy-bottomed skillet on the grill in the same way as on a conventional stove top and this is a good way to cook fish. Grease the surface and make sure the coals are very hot for a successful result.

Using skewers Firm fish, such as tuna, swordfish, or monkfish, is the best to use for kabobs. And, of course, seafood, such as shrimp, is delicious cooked this way too. Most skewered food is marinated first. Bamboo skewers need soaking before use and metal ones should be oiled.

Smoking To dry smoke, no water bath is needed and this is generally the method used for fish. The fish should first be soaked in salted water and then left out on a rack to dry completely, after which it is cooked a long time in a closed, or foil-tented grill over low coals .

Skinning flat fish (1)

Flat fish are usually skinned before filleting. Lay the fish dark side uppermost and head away from you. Make an incision in the skin across the bone where the tail joins the body. Working from the cut, loosen a flap of skin with a thumbnail or knife. Hold the tail firmly with one hand (a cloth or a little salt on your fingertips will help you to grip it) and pull the skin backwards towards the head, not up. When you have removed the skin as far as the jaws, turn the fish over and, holding it by the head, pull the skin until you reach the tail.

Filleting flat fish (2)

Place the fish with its head away from you, eyes facing up. With the point of a knife, slit along the backbone from head to tail. Insert the knife blade between the flesh and ribs to one side of the backbone, next to the head. With short, slicing movements, keeping the blade next to the ribs at a shallow angle, separate flesh from bones. Cut the fillet off at the tail and trim. Remove the other fillet on top of the bone, then turn the fish over and repeat.

Filleting round fish (3)

Round fish are usually skinned after filleting: you will get two fillets. Place the fish on its side and place the point of the knife beside the dorsal fin. Cut down along the backbone to the tail, keeping the blade just above the center of the backbone, but close to the upper bones of the rib cage. Cut from the dorsal fin to the head. Raise the top fillet slightly and, working from head to tail, work the fillet away from the ribs with a slicing motion of the blade. Slice along the backbone again, this time with the knife placed just below the center. Lift away the backbone and ribs from the fish.

Skinning fillets (4)

Lay the fillet skin side down on a work surface and make an incision through the flesh across the tail end. With the knife blade, loosen about half an inch of flesh. Grip the skin at the tail end (a little salt on your fingertips or a cloth will help you to grip it), slant the knife away from you, and work towards the head, slicing through the flesh, close to the skin, and pushing flesh away with the knife.

Whole Fish

Grilled Flounder with Hot Sauce

MAKES 2 SERVINGS

*1 FLOUNDER, WEIGHING ABOUT
1½ POUNDS*

SALT AND FRESHLY GROUND BLACK PEPPER

*1 TABLESPOON VEGETABLE OIL,
PLUS EXTRA FOR BRUSHING*

½ TEASPOON MINCED GARLIC

½ TEASPOON CHOPPED FRESH GINGER

2 SHALLOTS, FINELY CHOPPED

*2 OR 3 SMALL FRESH RED CHILIES,
SEEDED AND CHOPPED*

1 TABLESPOON CHOPPED SCALLION

2 TABLESPOONS FISH SAUCE

1 TEASPOON SUGAR

*1 TABLESPOON TAMARIND WATER
OR LIME JUICE*

*2 OR 3 TABLESPOONS CHICKEN STOCK
OR WATER*

2 TEASPOONS CORNSTARCH

◆ Score both sides of fish at 1-inch intervals and rub with salt and pepper. Let stand 25 minutes.

◆ Brush both sides of fish with oil and place on the rack over hot coals. Cook about 4 minutes on each side until lightly brown but not burnt. Place on a warmed serving dish.

◆ Heat 1 tablespoon oil in a small pan and stir-fry garlic, ginger, shallots, chilies, and scallion 1 minute.

◆ Add fish sauce, sugar, tamarind water or lime juice, and stock or water. Bring to a boil and simmer 30 seconds.

◆ Mix cornstarch with 1 tablespoon water and stir into sauce to thicken. Pour sauce over fish and serve.

Malaysian-style Flounder

MAKES 4 SERVINGS

*4 FLOUNDER, EACH WEIGHING
ABOUT 12 OUNCES*

*4 LARGE GARLIC CLOVES,
CUT INTO FINE SLIVERS*

*1-INCH PIECE FRESH GINGER,
CUT INTO FINE SLIVERS*

¼ CUP PEANUT OIL

¼ CUP LIGHT SOY SAUCE

1 TABLESPOON SESAME OIL

1 TABLESPOON RICE WINE

4 SCALLIONS, THINLY SLICED

◆ With the point of a sharp knife, cut 5 diagonal slashes, herringbone style, in both sides of each fish. Place fish in a shallow dish.

◆ Put garlic, ginger, peanut oil, soy sauce, sesame oil, and rice wine in a small pan. Heat to simmering point and pour over fish, spooning marinade into slashes. Refrigerate at least 1 hour, turning fish every 30 minutes.

◆ Lift fish from marinade and place on the rack of a prepared grill, preferably in rectangular, hinged wire baskets, pale skin side down. Cook about 2 minutes. Turn carefully and cook an additional 2 or 3 minutes, depending on thickness of fish.

◆ Reheat any remaining marinade and pour over fish. Sprinkle with scallions and serve.

Tandoori Trout

MAKES 2 SERVINGS

Seeds from 6 cardamom pods

2 teaspoons cumin seeds

¼ cup plain yogurt

1 large garlic clove, chopped

2 tablespoons lime juice

1-inch piece fresh ginger, chopped

1 teaspoon garam masala

Dash ground turmeric

¼ teaspoon cayenne

Salt

1 teaspoon red food coloring (optional)

2 trout, each weighing about 10 ounces

Vegetable oil for brushing

Rice with chilies and tomato and onion salad, to serve (optional)

Lemon and lime wedges and cilantro sprigs, to garnish (optional)

◆ Heat a small, heavy-bottomed pan. Add cardamom and cumin seeds and heat until fragrant. Place seeds in a mortar or small bowl and crush with a pestle or the end of a rolling pin.

◆ Place yogurt, garlic, lime juice, ginger, garam masala, turmeric, cayenne, and salt into a blender or small food processor and mix together to make a paste. Add food coloring, if desired.

◆ With the point of a sharp knife, make 3 deep slashes in each side of each trout. Spread spice mixture over trout, working it into slashes.

◆ Place trout into a shallow, nonmetallic dish in a single layer. Cover and let marinate in refrigerator 4 hours.

◆ Sprinkle a little oil over fish, place on the rack of a prepared grill, and cook about 7 minutes on each side.

◆ Serve with chili rice, and tomato and onion salad, garnished with lemon and lime wedges and cilantro sprigs, if desired.

Baked Trout with Thai Spices

MAKES 4 SERVINGS

4 MEDIUM TROUT

OIL FOR BRUSHING

RED CURRY PASTE

8 DRIED RED CHILIES,
SEEDED AND CHOPPED

8 CILANTRO ROOTS,
WASHED AND CHOPPED

1 TABLESPOON GRATED FRESH GINGER

2 LEMON GRASS STALKS, CHOPPED

4 KAFFIR LIME LEAVES, SHREDDED,
OR GRATED ZEST 2 LIMES

4 GARLIC CLOVES, CHOPPED

2 SHALLOTS, CHOPPED

SALT AND 1 TEASPOON GROUND
BLACK PEPPER

SAUCE

1 BUNCH SCALLIONS, CHOPPED

1/4 CUP DARK SOY SAUCE

1/4 CUP DRY SHERRY

JUICE 2 LIMES

2 TABLESPOONS CHOPPED
FRESH CILANTRO

◆ Wash and dry trout and cut 4 slashes in each side.

◆ To make curry paste, place dried chilies, cilantro roots, ginger, lemon grass, lime leaves, garlic, shallots, salt, and pepper in a blender and purée until smooth. Spread mixture all over inside and outside of trout.

◆ Lightly oil 4 sheets of heavy-duty aluminum foil and place a trout in the center of each one. Draw up edges of foil, leaving a gap at the top.

◆ To make sauce, combine scallions, soy sauce, sherry, 1/4 cup water, lime juice, and chopped cilantro in a bowl. Divide sauce between packages.

◆ Seal package edges by twisting foil, then place on the rack of a prepared grill and cook 20 to 25 minutes until trout are cooked through. Serve at once.

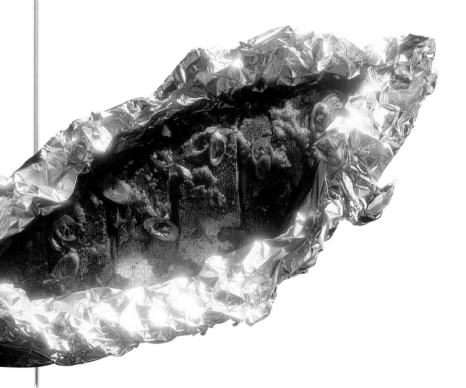

Red Mullet with Fennel

MAKES 6 SERVINGS

6 RED MULLET, EACH WEIGHING
ABOUT 6 OUNCES

2 SMALL FENNEL BULBS, THICKLY SLICED

1¼ CUPS OLIVE OIL

⅓ CUP DRY WHITE WINE

1 GARLIC CLOVE, ROUGHLY CHOPPED

1 SMALL RED CHILI, SEEDED AND CHOPPED

4 THYME SPRIGS, BRUISED

2 PARSLEY SPRIGS, BRUISED

1 TEASPOON CORIANDER SEEDS, CRUSHED

½ TEASPOON FENNEL SEEDS

SALT AND PEPPER

◆ Wash mullet inside and out and dry well. Cut 2 small slashes through the skin of each fish on both sides, and place in a large, shallow dish. Add fennel slices.

◆ Mix together olive oil, wine, garlic, chili, thyme, parsley, coriander and fennel seeds, and salt and pepper. Pour over fish, cover, and let marinate several hours, or overnight, turning fish and fennel in marinade occasionally.

◆ Remove fish and fennel from marinade. Grill fish 4 or 5 minutes on each side and fennel 2 or 3 minutes on each side until both are cooked and lightly charred. Baste with marinade if necessary.

◆ Serve immediately, with crusty bread and a crisp green salad, if desired.

Smoked Red Snapper

MAKES 4 TO 6 SERVINGS

2 RED SNAPPER, EACH WEIGHING ABOUT
1 TO 1½ POUNDS

⅓ CUP SEA SALT

2 HANDFULS HICKORY CHIPS

OLIVE OIL

◆ Put fish in a large shallow glass or plastic dish. Dissolve salt in 4 cups cold water. Pour over fish and let soak at least 30 minutes.

◆ Drain fish thoroughly. Put on wire rack and leave in an airy room about 2½ hours until dry. Fish must be dry to touch before being smoked. Meanwhile, soak hickory chips in water 30 minutes.

◆ Using a covered grill, light coals and push to one side (fish must not be placed directly over coals). Wait until burned down to white ash stage, then add drained hickory chips.

◆ Thoroughly brush each fish with oil and place on the grill rack away from coals. Close lid and grill fish 30 to 45 minutes, turning once, or until flesh flakes when tested with a knife.

Mullet with Anchovy Sauce

MAKES 4 SERVINGS

*4 RED MULLET, EACH WEIGHING
ABOUT 8 OUNCES*

*4 CANNED ANCHOVY FILLETS, RINSED AND
CUT INTO 4 PIECES EACH*

ALL-PURPOSE FLOUR FOR COATING

SALT AND FRESHLY GROUND BLACK PEPPER

OIL FOR BRUSHING

*CHOPPED FRESH PARSLEY, CAPERS, AND
1 ORANGE, PEELED AND DIVIDED INTO
SEGMENTS, TO GARNISH*

ANCHOVY SAUCE

½ CUP FRESHLY SQUEEZED ORANGE JUICE

*¼ CUP SKINNED, SEEDED, AND
CHOPPED TOMATO*

*4 CANNED ANCHOVY FILLETS, RINSED AND
ROUGHLY CHOPPED*

PEPPER, TO TASTE

◆ Using the point of a sharp knife, cut 2 diagonal slashes in both sides of each fish. Insert a piece of anchovy fillet in each slash.

◆ Season flour with salt and pepper, then coat fish lightly and evenly. Brush fish with oil.

◆ Place fish on a rack over hot coals and cook until crisp, about 5 minutes each side. Transfer to a serving plate and keep warm.

◆ To make sauce, put orange juice, tomato, anchovies, and pepper into a pan. Boil gently until thickened to a light sauce. Add water if necessary.

◆ Serve fish with sauce and garnish with parsley, capers, and orange segments.

Grilled Gray Mullet

MAKES 6 SERVINGS

*1 GRAY MULLET, WEIGHING ABOUT
3½ POUNDS*

SALT AND FRESHLY GROUND BLACK PEPPER

1 BAY LEAF

1 ROSEMARY SPRIG

⅓ CUP OLIVE OIL

JUICE 2 SMALL LEMONS

1 TEASPOON DRIED OREGANO

1 TABLESPOON CHOPPED FRESH PARSLEY

2 GARLIC CLOVES, FINELY CHOPPED

*BAY LEAVES AND LEMON WEDGES,
TO SERVE*

◆ Season cavity of fish with salt and pepper. Place bay leaf and rosemary inside fish.

◆ Place mullet on the rack of a prepared grill over medium coals and cook about 10 minutes on each side.

◆ In a bowl, whisk together olive oil, lemon juice, oregano, parsley, and garlic until thick.

◆ Lay fish on a serving platter and garnish with bay leaves and lemon wedges. Pour sauce over fish and serve at once.

Spiced Sweet and Sour Fish

MAKES 4 OR 5 SERVINGS

1 TABLESPOON CUMIN SEEDS

1 TEASPOON CORIANDER SEEDS

3 TABLESPOONS VEGETABLE OIL

½ FRESH RED CHILI, SEEDED AND FINELY CHOPPED

3 GARLIC CLOVES, SMASHED

2 ONIONS, CHOPPED

1-INCH PIECE SHRIMP PASTE, ROASTED (SEE NOTE)

¼ CUP LIME JUICE

3 TABLESPOONS DARK SOY SAUCE

BROWN SUGAR, TO TASTE

2 WHOLE FISH, EACH WEIGHING ABOUT 1½ POUNDS

◆ Heat cumin and coriander seeds in a skillet over medium-high heat until toasted with a fragrant roasted aroma. Cool slightly, then grind in a small blender or using a mortar and pestle.

◆ Heat oil in a small skillet over medium-high heat. Add chili, garlic, and onions and fry until lightly browned. Tip into blender containing cumin and coriander.

◆ Add shrimp paste, lime juice, and soy sauce and mix to a thin paste. Add ½ cup hot water, and brown sugar to taste. Set aside.

◆ Cut 3 deep slashes on both sides of each fish and score along backbone. Place on the rack of a prepared grill.

◆ Cook about 6 or 7 minutes on each side. Flesh should just flake when tested with the point of a sharp knife, and skin should be brown.

◆ Reheat sauce, pour some over fish, and serve remainder separately.

Note: To roast shrimp paste, hold it in tongs over a naked flame, turning it so it roasts evenly.

Trout in Vine Leaves

MAKES 4 SERVINGS

4 TROUT

2 TABLESPOONS OLIVE OIL

GRATED ZEST 1 SEVILLE ORANGE

2 TABLESPOONS FRESHLY SQUEEZED ORANGE JUICE

1 GARLIC CLOVE, CRUSHED

SEEDS FROM 6 CARDAMOM PODS, CRUSHED

½ TEASPOON SALT

½ TEASPOON BLACK PEPPER

1 TEASPOON DIJON-STYLE MUSTARD

2 BAY LEAVES

3 TEASPOONS CHOPPED FENNEL

8 VINE LEAVES

1 TEASPOON ARROWROOT

FENNEL SPRIGS AND BAY LEAVES, TO GARNISH

◆ Rinse fish under running water and dry on absorbent kitchen paper. Score flesh on each side.

◆ To make marinade, mix together olive oil, orange zest and juice, garlic, cardamom seeds, salt, pepper, mustard, bay leaves, and fennel.

◆ Immerse fish in marinade and turn to coat evenly. Cover with plastic wrap and leave in a cool place to marinate 1 hour.

◆ Take fish out of marinade, reserving marinade, and loosely wrap each fish in 2 vine leaves.

◆ Arrange fish on the rack of a preheated grill and cook about 6 minutes on each side. Unwrap fish and arrange on individual plates.

◆ Blend remaining marinade with arrowroot. Put in a saucepan and bring to a boil, stirring. Cook 1 minute, until thickened and glossy.

◆ Pour sauce over fish and garnish with fennel sprigs and bay leaves.

Variation: Use 8 small red mullet instead of trout.

Bass with Fennel

MAKES 6 SERVINGS

1 BASS, WEIGHING ABOUT 6¾ POUNDS

1 BUNCH FENNEL

SALT AND FRESHLY GROUND BLACK PEPPER

JUICE 1 LEMON

3 TABLESPOONS OLIVE OIL

*LIME SLICES AND FENNEL SPRIGS,
TO GARNISH*

◆ With a sharp knife, cut deep diagonal slashes in each side of fish and insert a fennel sprig into each slash. Season fish inside and out with salt and pepper and put 2 or 3 fennel sprigs in cavity.

◆ Mix together lemon juice and oil. Brush over top half of fish and sprinkle a little inside fish.

◆ Place fish on the preheated grill rack, brushed side down, and lay a fennel sprig on top. Cook 10 to 12 minutes until bottom half is cooked and skin is lightly charred.

◆ Turn over fish carefully, brush with lemon juice and oil, and place another fennel sprig on top. Cook an additional 10 to 12 minutes, until cooked through.

◆ Cut into portions, garnish with lime slices and fennel sprigs, and serve.

Fillets
and Steaks

Flounder with Wild Mushroom Sauce

MAKES 4 SERVINGS

2 TABLESPOONS DRIED PORCINI
MUSHROOMS

1/4 CUP BRANDY

2/3 CUP VEGETABLE STOCK

1/4 CUP OLIVE OIL

2 SHALLOTS, CHOPPED

8 OUNCES MIXED WILD MUSHROOMS
(E.G. CHANTERELLES, PORCINI, BLEWITS,
OYSTER), CHOPPED IF LARGE

4 FLOUNDER FILLETS

1/2 STICK UNSALTED BUTTER, SOFTENED

SALT AND PEPPER

1 TABLESPOON CHOPPED FRESH PARSLEY

◆ Soak dried porcini mushrooms in 2/3 cup boiling water 30 minutes. Strain, reserving liquid, and chop porcini mushrooms.

◆ Place reserved mushroom stock, brandy, and vegetable stock in a pan. Bring to a boil, reduce heat, and simmer to reduce until only about 1/3 cup remains. Set aside.

◆ In a pan, fry shallots in 2 tablespoons olive oil 3 minutes. Add fresh and soaked mushrooms and stir-fry 5 minutes. Cover and keep warm.

◆ Brush fish fillets with remaining oil, place on the rack of a prepared grill, and cook about 2 or 3 minutes on each side until cooked.

◆ Meanwhile, bring reduced stock to a rolling boil. Whisk in butter, a little at a time, until sauce is thickened and glossy. Season to taste.

◆ Transfer fish to warmed plates, spoon over mushrooms, and pour over sauce. Sprinkle with parsley and serve at once.

Fillet of Turbot with Braised Leeks

MAKES 4 SERVINGS

2 TABLESPOONS BUTTER

2 SHALLOTS, QUARTERED

2 TEASPOONS YELLOW MUSTARD SEEDS

1 POUND BABY LEEKS, THINLY SLICED

1/4 CUP DRY SHERRY

2 TABLESPOONS CHOPPED FRESH CHERVIL

SALT AND PEPPER

4 SMALL TURBOT FILLETS

1 TABLESPOON OLIVE OIL

BABY POTATOES AND CARROTS, TO SERVE
(OPTIONAL)

◆ Melt butter in a pan, add shallots and mustard seeds, and fry 3 minutes. Add leeks and fry an additional 3 minutes.

◆ Add sherry, cover, and cook over a low heat 5 to 8 minutes until leeks are tender. Stir in chervil and season to taste.

◆ Meanwhile, wash turbot fillets and pat dry. Brush with a little oil and place on the rack of a prepared grill 3 to 4 minutes on each side until cooked through.

◆ Serve turbot on a bed of braised leeks, with baby potatoes and carrots, if desired.

Note: Turbot is an expensive fish and may be difficult to find, but its delicate flavor works well with leeks. Flounder makes a good substitute.

Grilled Fish with Cilantro

1½ POUNDS GRAY MULLET OR
MONKFISH FILLETS

3 TABLESPOONS OLIVE OIL

2 GARLIC CLOVES, CRUSHED

2 TEASPOONS CUMIN SEEDS,
TOASTED AND GROUND

1 TEASPOON PAPRIKA

1 FRESH GREEN CHILI, SEEDED AND
FINELY CHOPPED

HANDFUL CILANTRO LEAVES,
FINELY CHOPPED

3 TABLESPOONS LIME JUICE

SALT

HOT COOKED RICE, TO SERVE (OPTIONAL)

MINT SPRIGS AND LIME WEDGES,
TO GARNISH

◆ Place fish into a shallow nonmetallic dish. In a bowl mix together olive oil, garlic, cumin, paprika, chili, cilantro, lime juice, and salt.

◆ Spoon marinade over fish. Cover and refrigerate 3 or 4 hours, turning fish in marinade occasionally.

◆ Remove fish from marinade and place on the rack of a prepared grill. Cook about 4 minutes on each side, basting with cilantro mixture occasionally, until flesh flakes when tested with the point of a sharp knife.

◆ Serve fish warm on a bed of rice, if desired, and garnish with mint sprigs and lime wedges.

Bass with Ginger and Lime

2 SHALLOTS, FINELY CHOPPED

½-INCH PIECE FRESH GINGER, FINELY CHOPPED

JUICE 2 LIMES

¼ CUP RICE WINE VINEGAR

1 CUP OLIVE OIL

2 TABLESPOONS CHINESE SESAME OIL

2 TABLESPOONS SOY SAUCE

SALT AND PEPPER

6 TO 8 BASS FILLETS, EACH WEIGHING ABOUT 6 OUNCES AND ABOUT ½ INCH THICK

BUNCH FRESH CILANTRO

TOASTED SESAME SEEDS, TO GARNISH

◆ In a bowl mix together shallots, ginger, lime juice, rice wine vinegar, olive and sesame oils, soy sauce, salt, and pepper.

◆ Brush fish lightly with ginger mixture and place on the rack of a prepared grill. Cook 2 or 3 minutes on each side, basting occasionally with ginger mixture.

◆ Before serving, place remaining ginger mixture in a pan, bring to a boil, then remove from the heat.

◆ Chop cilantro leaves and discard stalks. Reserve a few whole leaves for garnish. Mix chopped cilantro into ginger mixture.

◆ Spoon some sauce onto serving plates, then place grilled fish on top.

◆ Sprinkle with sesame seeds and garnish with cilantro leaves to serve.

Sesame-coated Whiting

MAKES 4 SERVINGS

1 TABLESPOON DIJON-STYLE MUSTARD

1 TABLESPOON TOMATO PASTE

1½ TEASPOONS FINELY CHOPPED FRESH TARRAGON

SQUEEZE LEMON JUICE

PEPPER

½ CUP SESAME SEEDS

2 TABLESPOONS ALL-PURPOSE FLOUR

1 EGG, LIGHTLY BEATEN

4 WHITING FILLETS, EACH WEIGHING ABOUT 5 OUNCES, SKINNED

OLIVE OIL FOR BRUSHING

TARRAGON SPRIGS AND LEMON WEDGES, TO GARNISH (OPTIONAL)

◆ In a small bowl mix together mustard, tomato paste, tarragon, lemon juice, and pepper.

◆ Combine sesame seeds and flour and spread evenly on a large plate. Pour beaten egg into a shallow bowl.

◆ Spread mustard mixture over both sides of each fish fillet, then dip fillet in egg. Coat fish evenly in sesame seeds and flour mixture, then refrigerate 30 minutes.

◆ Place coated fillets on the rack of a prepared grill (ideally in hinged wire baskets). Brush one side of each fillet lightly with oil, then cook 2 or 3 minutes. Turn fish over, lightly brush top with oil, and cook an additional 2 or 3 minutes.

◆ Transfer fish to a warm serving plate to serve and garnish with lemon wedges and tarragon sprigs, if desired.

Cod with Teriyaki Glaze

MAKES 4 SERVINGS

2 TABLESPOONS SOY SAUCE

*1 TABLESPOON RICE WINE OR
MEDIUM-DRY SHERRY*

1 TABLESPOON LIGHT SOFT BROWN SUGAR

1 TEASPOON GRATED FRESH GINGER

4 COD FILLETS WITH SKIN

CHERVIL SPRIGS, TO GARNISH

*STIR-FRIED VEGETABLES, TO SERVE
(OPTIONAL)*

◆ To make teriyaki glaze, gently heat together soy sauce, rice wine or sherry, sugar, and ginger 2 or 3 minutes in a small saucepan until lightly syrupy. Let cool.

◆ Brush both sides of fish fillets with teriyaki glaze. Place on the rack of a preheated grill and cook 3 or 4 minutes on each side.

◆ Transfer fish to warm serving plates. Reheat any remaining glaze and pour over fish. Garnish with chervil sprigs and serve with stir-fried vegetables, if desired.

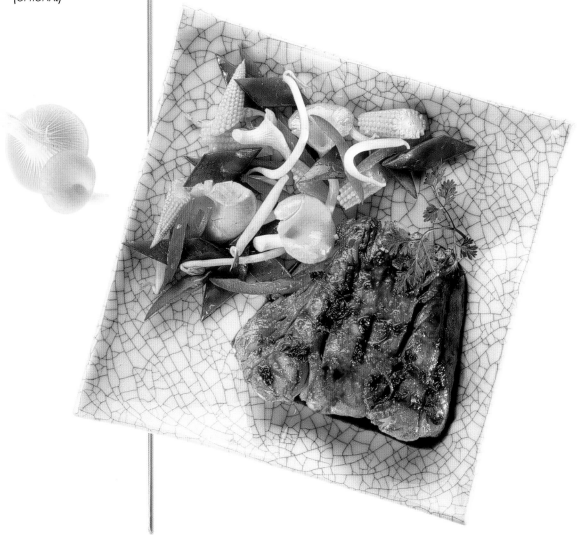

Tuna with Tomato and Olive Salsa

¼ cup green olive purée

½ cup olive oil

3 garlic cloves, crushed

4 tuna steaks, each weighing about 5 ounces

TOMATO AND OLIVE SALSA

15 black olives, pitted and sliced

4 tomatoes, peeled, seeded, and sliced

¾ cup sun-dried tomatoes in oil, drained and sliced

4 scallions

14 basil leaves, torn

Dash sugar

◆ To make marinade, mix together in a shallow dish green olive purée, olive oil, and garlic. Season with salt and pepper.

◆ Add tuna steaks to marinade and turn to coat evenly. Cover and refrigerate 2 hours.

◆ To make salsa, combine black olives, tomatoes, sun-dried tomatoes, scallions, basil leaves, and sugar. Refrigerate until required.

◆ Remove tuna steaks from marinade, reserving marinade for basting. Cook steaks on a prepared grill about 5 minutes on each side, basting occasionally.

◆ Serve grilled tuna at once with salsa.

Mesquite-smoked Monkfish

½ cup extra virgin olive oil

¼ cup white wine vinegar

4 garlic cloves, crushed

2 teaspoons black peppercorns, crushed

2 teaspoons chopped fennel fronds

Dash sea salt

4 pieces monkfish tail with the bone, each weighing about 7 ounces

about 1 cup mesquite chips, soaked in cold water 1 hour

Cooked new potatoes, to serve (optional)

◆ To make marinade, mix olive oil, white wine vinegar, garlic, peppercorns, chopped fennel fronds, and salt together in a bowl.

◆ Place fish portions in a shallow dish and pour over marinade, turning fish to coat evenly. Cover and refrigerate 2 hours.

◆ Drain soaked mesquite chips and sprinkle over the hot coals of a prepared grill.

◆ Remove fish from marinade, reserving marinade for basting. Cook fish on the grill about 15 minutes, or until cooked through, turning and basting occasionally.

◆ Serve at once, with new potatoes, if desired.

Salmon with Ginger Dip

MAKES 4 SERVINGS

*4 SALMON FILLETS, EACH WEIGHING
ABOUT 6 OUNCES, SKINNED*

3 TABLESPOONS LIGHT SOY SAUCE

1 TABLESPOON DRY SHERRY

*1-INCH PIECE FRESH GINGER, PEELED AND
CUT INTO THIN STRIPS*

FRESHLY GROUND BLACK PEPPER

2 TABLESPOONS SWEET SHERRY

4 SCALLIONS, SHREDDED, TO GARNISH

*LIGHTLY COOKED ASPARAGUS TIPS,
TO SERVE (OPTIONAL)*

◆ Using a sharp knife, lightly score top of salmon fillets in diagonal lines, taking care not to slice all the way through.

◆ Place salmon in a shallow dish. Mix together 2 tablespoons soy sauce, dry sherry, and ginger strips and spoon over salmon. Cover and refrigerate 1 hour.

◆ Remove salmon from marinade, season with pepper, and place on an oiled grill rack. Cook 2 or 3 minutes on each side.

◆ Meanwhile, make dip by mixing together sweet sherry and remaining 1 tablespoon soy sauce.

◆ Drain cooked salmon on absorbent kitchen paper and place on serving plates. Garnish with shredded scallions and serve with dip, accompanied by asparagus tips, if desired.

Cod with Vinegar Sauce

MAKES 4 SERVINGS

1 TABLESPOON SUNFLOWER OIL

6 SHALLOTS, SLICED

2 TABLESPOONS WHITE RICE VINEGAR

2 TEASPOONS SUGAR

1 TABLESPOON LIGHT SOY SAUCE

1¼ CUPS VEGETABLE STOCK

*1 TEASPOON CORNSTARCH MIXED WITH
2 TEASPOONS WATER*

*4 COD STEAKS, EACH WEIGHING
ABOUT 6 OUNCES*

SALT AND FRESHLY GROUND PEPPER

2 TABLESPOONS CHOPPED FRESH CHIVES

◆ Heat half the oil in a pan and stir-fry shallots 2 or 3 minutes. Add vinegar, sugar, and soy sauce and stir-fry 1 minute.

◆ Pour in stock and bring to a boil. Simmer 8 or 9 minutes, or until thickened and slightly reduced. Stir in cornstarch mixture and cook, stirring, until thickened. Keep warm.

◆ Season cod steaks on both sides and place on the rack of a prepared grill. Brush with remaining oil and grill about 4 minutes on each side, or until cooked. Drain on absorbent kitchen paper, then remove skin.

◆ Stir chives into vinegar sauce, spoon over cod steaks, and serve.

Halibut Chargrilled in Banana Leaves

MAKES 4 SERVINGS

1 POUND SKINLESS, BONELESS HALIBUT, CUT INTO 1-INCH CUBES

4 PIECES BANANA LEAF, EACH ABOUT 12 INCHES SQUARE (SEE NOTE)

OIL FOR BRUSHING

SPICY PASTE

1 LARGE DRIED CHILI

2-INCH PIECE GALANGAL, PEELED AND CHOPPED (SEE NOTE)

2 LEMON GRASS STALKS, FINELY CHOPPED

2 GARLIC CLOVES, CRUSHED

1 SHALLOT, FINELY CHOPPED

2 KAFFIR LIME LEAVES, FINELY CHOPPED

1 TABLESPOON THAI FISH SAUCE

3 TABLESPOONS PEANUT OIL

Note: Galangal is used for its exotic taste, but you can substitute fresh ginger. Heavy-duty aluminum foil can be used instead of banana leaves; it will not need oiling.

◆ Prepare spicy paste. Soak red chili in hot water 10 minutes, then drain and chop finely.

◆ Place chili, galangal, lemon grass, garlic, shallot, lime leaves, fish sauce, and oil in a spice grinder or food processor and blend to a smooth paste.

◆ Transfer spicy paste to a shallow glass dish, add cubed fish, and toss to coat evenly. Cover and refrigerate 2 hours.

◆ Brush banana leaves with a little oil and divide marinated fish between them. Wrap up to form packages and secure with toothpicks.

◆ Brush outside of packages with a little oil and cook on a prepared grill about 10 minutes, until fish is cooked through.

Fish Gratins

MAKES 4 SERVINGS

½ TEASPOON DIJON-STYLE MUSTARD

1 TABLESPOON LEMON JUICE

1 TABLESPOON OLIVE OIL

DASH FRESHLY GRATED NUTMEG

SALT AND PEPPER

4 COD OR HADDOCK STEAKS, EACH
WEIGHING ABOUT 5 OUNCES

½ CUP FINELY SHREDDED SHARP
CHEDDAR CHEESE

3 TABLESPOONS FRESHLY GRATED
PARMESAN CHEESE

2 TABLESPOONS FINE FRESH BREADCRUMBS

PAPRIKA

◆ In a small bowl using a fork, beat together mustard and lemon juice, then gradually whisk in oil. Add nutmeg and season with salt and pepper.

◆ Cut squares of heavy-duty aluminum foil large enough to contain each fish fillet. Coat fillets in mustard mixture, then place on squares of foil.

◆ Cover fish with shredded Cheddar cheese. Mix together Parmesan cheese and breadcrumbs, sprinkle evenly onto fish, then season generously with pepper.

◆ Turn edges of foil over and pinch at the tops to seal. Place foil packages on the rack of a preheated grill 8 or 10 minutes until fish is cooked through and cheese has melted.

◆ Open packages and lightly sprinkle fish with paprika to serve.

Middle Eastern Monkfish

2 GARLIC CLOVES, FINELY CHOPPED

2½-INCH PIECE FRESH GINGER, FINELY CHOPPED

3 TABLESPOONS OLIVE OIL

2½ TABLESPOONS TOMATO PASTE

1½ TEASPOONS GROUND CINNAMON

1 TEASPOON CARAWAY SEEDS, CRUSHED

SALT AND PEPPER

2¼ POUNDS MONKFISH TAIL

½ SPANISH ONION, FINELY CHOPPED

COUSCOUS AND LEMON SLICES, TO SERVE (OPTIONAL)

◆ In a small bowl mix together garlic, ginger, olive oil, tomato paste, cinnamon, caraway seeds, salt, and pepper.

◆ Remove fine skin from monkfish, then spread with spice mixture. Place fish in a shallow dish, cover, and leave in a cool place 1½ hours.

◆ Cut a piece of heavy-duty aluminum foil large enough to enclose fish. Make a bed of chopped onion on foil and place monkfish and remaining spice paste on top. Fold foil loosely over fish and seal edges tightly.

◆ Cook on the rack of a prepared grill about 20 to 25 minutes. Open foil, baste fish with spice paste, reseal, turn package over, and cook an additional 10 to 15 minutes as necessary.

◆ Serve monkfish on a bed of couscous and garnish with lemon slices, if desired.

Tuna with Ginger Vinaigrette

MAKES 4 SERVINGS

1-INCH PIECE FRESH GINGER, FINELY CHOPPED

2 LARGE SCALLIONS, WHITE AND SOME GREEN PARTS, FINELY SLICED

1 CUP OLIVE OIL

JUICE 2 LIMES

2 TABLESPOONS SOY SAUCE

2 TABLESPOONS SESAME OIL

1 BUNCH CILANTRO, A FEW SPRIGS RESERVED FOR GARNISH, REMAINDER FINELY CHOPPED

PEPPER

6 TUNA STEAKS, EACH WEIGHING ABOUT 5 OR 6 OUNCES

◆ To make ginger vinaigrette, in a bowl stir together ginger, scallions, olive oil, lime juice, and soy sauce, then whisk in sesame oil. Add chopped cilantro and season with pepper. Set aside.

◆ Place tuna steaks on the rack of a prepared grill and cook about 3 or 4 minutes on each side.

◆ Spoon some dressing onto 6 individual serving plates. Add tuna steaks and garnish with cilantro sprigs. Serve any remaining dressing separately.

Salmon with Capers and Gazpacho Salsa

MAKES 4 SERVINGS

3 TABLESPOONS OLIVE OIL

GRATED ZEST AND JUICE 1 LIME

1 TABLESPOON CAPERS IN BRINE, DRAINED

4 SALMON STEAKS

GAZPACHO SALSA

4 TOMATOES, PEELED, SEEDED, AND DICED

½ LARGE CUCUMBER, DICED

½ ONION, DICED

½ RED BELL PEPPER, DICED

1 TABLESPOON EACH CHOPPED FRESH PARSLEY AND CILANTRO

1 TEASPOON CASTER SUGAR

2 TABLESPOONS RED WINE VINEGAR

◆ In a bowl mix together olive oil, lime zest and juice, capers, and a dash of salt. Place salmon steaks in a shallow dish and pour over marinade. Cover and refrigerate salmon 2 hours, if time permits.

◆ To make salsa, put diced tomatoes, cucumber, onion, and bell pepper in a bowl with chopped parsley and cilantro, sugar, and wine vinegar. Season to taste with salt and pepper. Cover and refrigerate until required.

◆ Remove salmon steaks from marinade and press a few capers into the flesh of each piece. Reserve remaining marinade for basting.

◆ Cook salmon on a prepared grill 4 or 5 minutes on each side, basting occasionally with marinade.

◆ Serve salmon hot with gazpacho salsa.

Pan-fried Fish with Lemon and Garlic Sauce

MAKES 6 SERVINGS

6 SWORDFISH, HALIBUT, OR SALMON STEAKS

1 CUP OLIVE OIL

12 BAY LEAVES, BRUISED

3 CARDAMOM PODS, BRUISED

1 TABLESPOON CHOPPED FRESH PARSLEY

1 TABLESPOON GROUND PAPRIKA

6 LEMON SLICES

JUICE 1 LEMON

1 GARLIC CLOVE, CRUSHED

1 TABLESPOON CHOPPED FRESH PARSLEY

SALT AND CAYENNE

◆ Wash and dry fish steaks and place in a large shallow dish.

◆ In a bowl mix together ⅔ cup olive oil, bay leaves, cardamom pods, chopped parsley, paprika, and lemon slices. Pour over fish, cover, and marinate 2 to 3 hours, turning fish in marinade occasionally.

◆ To make sauce, beat lemon juice with remaining olive oil until thickened. Add garlic, parsley, salt, and cayenne.

◆ Place a griddle on the grill, brush with oil, and allow it to get really hot. Fry fish on both sides 4 to 6 minutes, until golden and firm to the touch. Alternatively, place fish directly over the heat on the grill and cook 4 to 6 minutes on each side.

◆ Serve fish steaks with plenty of lemon and garlic sauce poured over.

Aromatic Grilled Salmon

MAKES 6 SERVINGS

*6 MIDDLE-CUT SALMON CUTLETS,
EACH WEIGHING ABOUT 6 OUNCES
AND ¾ INCH THICK*

SALT AND FRESHLY GROUND BLACK PEPPER

ALL-PURPOSE FLOUR FOR COATING

1 STICK BUTTER

*HANDFUL FRESH WINTER SAVORY OR
1 OR 2 TABLESPOONS DRIED WINTER
SAVORY, MOISTENED*

6 TEASPOONS LUMPFISH CAVIAR

*WINTER SAVORY OR TARRAGON,
TO GARNISH*

◆ Rinse salmon and pat dry on absorbent kitchen paper. Season to taste with salt and pepper. Dip in flour and shake off surplus.

◆ Melt butter and brush over salmon steaks. Place in a rectangular hinged basket. Sprinkle winter savory over the coals when they are hot.

◆ Grill fish on rack over hot coals 4 or 5 minutes on each side, basting occasionally with melted butter. If cutlets start to brown too quickly, reduce heat, or move basket to side of grill. Cutlets are cooked when it is easy to move center bone.

◆ Serve salmon cutlets sprinkled with lumpfish caviar and garnished with winter savory or tarragon leaves.

Spiced Fish in Banana Leaves

MAKES 4 SERVINGS

1¼ POUNDS WHITE FISH FILLETS

BANANA LEAVES

OIL FOR BRUSHING

SPICE PASTE

6 SHALLOTS, CHOPPED

2 GARLIC CLOVES, SMASHED

2 FRESH RED CHILIES, CORED, SEEDED, AND CHOPPED

1-INCH PIECE FRESH GINGER, CHOPPED

4 CANDLENUTS OR CASHEWS

½ TEASPOON TAMARIND PASTE

2 TEASPOONS GROUND CORIANDER

2 TEASPOONS GROUND CUMIN

¼ TEASPOON GROUND TURMERIC

DASH SALT

◆ To make spice paste, put shallots, garlic, chilies, ginger, nuts, tamarind paste, coriander, cumin, turmeric, and salt into a blender or food processor and mix to a paste.

◆ Cut fish into 4 x 2 x ½-inch pieces. Coat the top of each piece thickly with spice paste.

◆ If using banana leaves, hold them with tongs over a flame to soften. Oil leaves thoroughly and cut into pieces to wrap around pieces of fish. Secure packages with toothpicks. Alternatively, if banana leaves are not available, wrap fish in pieces of heavy-duty aluminum foil.

◆ Place fish packages on grill and cook 4 or 5 minutes on each side.

◆ Serve with lime wedges, and with banana leaf or foil partially torn away to reveal fish inside.

Blackened Sea Bass with Butter Sauce

*4 SEA BASS FILLETS, EACH WEIGHING
ABOUT 5 OUNCES*

½ STICK BUTTER, MELTED

LEMON WEDGES, TO SERVE

*SKEWERED NEW POTATOES, TO SERVE
(SEE NOTE)*

SPICE MIX

1 TEASPOON SALT

1 TEASPOON GARLIC GRANULES

1 TEASPOON DRIED PARSLEY

1 TEASPOON CHILI POWDER

½ TEASPOON GROUND BAY LEAVES

1 TABLESPOON CAYENNE

GROUND BLACK PEPPER

BUTTER SAUCE

3 TABLESPOONS DRY WHITE WINE

2 TABLESPOONS WHITE WINE VINEGAR

½ STICK BUTTER, DICED

⅔ CUP HEAVY CREAM

1 TABLESPOON CHOPPED FRESH PARSLEY

1 TABLESPOON CHOPPED FRESH CHIVES

◆ To make spice mix, in a bowl combine salt, garlic granules, dried parsley, chili powder, ground bay leaves, cayenne, and black pepper. Transfer to a plate.

◆ Brush sea bass fillets all over with melted butter, then place on spice mix and turn to coat evenly. Cover and refrigerate fillets 1 hour.

◆ Cook fish fillets on the oiled rack of a prepared grill 3 or 4 minutes on each side.

◆ Just before serving, make sauce. Place wine and vinegar in a saucepan and boil rapidly 1 or 2 minutes to reduce by half.

◆ Whisk in butter, a piece at a time, over low heat. Add cream and whisk 1 or 2 minutes, then stir in chopped parsley and chives.

◆ Serve sea bass with hot butter sauce and lemon wedges, accompanied by skewered new potatoes, if desired.

Note: To make skewered new potatoes, cook 16 baby new potatoes in boiling salted water about 12 minutes. Toss in plenty of olive oil, salt, and pepper while still warm, then thread onto 4 skewers and cook on the grill 12 to 15 minutes, turning frequently.

Chargrilled Tuna Niçoise

MAKES 4 SERVINGS

12 OUNCES WAXY NEW POTATOES, SCRAPED

4 OUNCES GREEN BEANS, HALVED

4 TUNA STEAKS, EACH WEIGHING ABOUT 6 OUNCES

1 ROMAINE LETTUCE

HANDFUL ARUGULA LEAVES

8 OUNCES CHERRY TOMATOES, HALVED

8 QUAILS' EGGS, HARD-BOILED AND HALVED

2-OUNCE CAN ANCHOVIES IN OLIVE OIL, DRAINED

12 BLACK OLIVES

VINAIGRETTE

½ TEASPOON DIJON-STYLE MUSTARD

1 TABLESPOON WHITE WINE VINEGAR

SALT AND FRESHLY GROUND BLACK PEPPER

½ CUP EXTRA VIRGIN OLIVE OIL

1 TABLESPOON CHOPPED FRESH CHIVES

◆ To make vinaigrette, whisk together mustard, vinegar, salt, and pepper. Whisk in olive oil, then stir in chives. Set aside.

◆ Cook potatoes in boiling, salted water 15 minutes, until tender. Drain, slice, and return to pan. Add 1 tablespoon of vinaigrette to potatoes, mix gently, and let cool.

◆ Cook beans in boiling salted water 3 or 4 minutes until tender but still crisp. Drain, rinse under cold water, and drain again. Add beans to potatoes and mix together.

◆ Brush tuna steaks on both sides with vinaigrette. Place on the rack of a prepared grill and cook 4 or 5 minutes on each side until browned but still slightly pink in the center.

◆ Meanwhile, arrange lettuce leaves and arugula on serving plates. Drizzle with a little vinaigrette. Arrange cooked potatoes and beans, tomatoes, hard-boiled eggs, anchovies, and olives on top.

◆ Place a tuna steak on top of each plate of salad, pour over remaining vinaigrette, and serve.

Oily Fish

Stuffed Sardines

MAKES 4 TO 6 SERVINGS

2 CUPS TRIMMED SPINACH LEAVES, WASHED

1 GARLIC CLOVE, CRUSHED

GRATED ZEST 1 LEMON

2 TABLESPOONS CHOPPED FRESH PARSLEY

1/4 CUP PINE NUTS, TOASTED AND CHOPPED

2 TABLESPOONS RAISINS

8 ANCHOVY FILLETS CANNED IN OIL,
DRAINED AND CHOPPED

1 CUP FRESH BREADCRUMBS

1/2 CUP FETA CHEESE, CRUMBLED

1/4 TEASPOON GROUND MIXED SPICE

2 TABLESPOONS OLIVE OIL

12 SARDINES, EACH WEIGHING
ABOUT 4 OUNCES

SALT AND PEPPER

LEMON WEDGES, TO GARNISH

◆ Place washed spinach leaves in a pan with no extra water and heat 2 or 3 minutes until just wilted. Drain, squeeze out excess liquid, and chop finely.

◆ In a bowl, mix together garlic, lemon zest, parsley, pine nuts, raisins, anchovies, breadcrumbs, feta, mixed spice, and 1 tablespoon olive oil. Stir in wilted spinach and set aside 1 hour to allow flavors to infuse.

◆ Wash and dry sardines and fill stomach cavities with spinach mixture. Brush with remaining oil and place on the prepared grill. Cook about 4 or 5 minutes on each side until browned and firm to the touch.

◆ Serve hot with lemon wedges.

Tarama Sardines

MAKES 6 SERVINGS

6 SARDINES

2 TABLESPOONS LEMON JUICE

FRESHLY GROUND BLACK PEPPER

3 OR 4 TABLESPOONS TARAMASALATA

PARSLEY SPRIGS, TO GARNISH

◆ Rinse sardines and pat dry on absorbent kitchen paper. Brush insides with lemon juice and season to taste with black pepper. Carefully fill cavities with taramasalata.

◆ Place sardines in a hinged rectangular basket and grill over hot coals 3 or 4 minutes on each side.

◆ Serve garnished with parsley sprigs.

Variation: Use small trout if sardines are not available and double the quantity of taramasalata.

Herrings in Oats

MAKES 4 SERVINGS

4 HERRINGS, EACH WEIGHING ABOUT 8 OUNCES, HEADS AND TAILS REMOVED

SALT AND PEPPER

1 LEMON, HALVED

⅔ CUP STEEL-CUT OATS

LEMON WEDGES, TO SERVE

MUSTARD SAUCE

⅓ CUP THICK MAYONNAISE

⅓ CUP PLAIN YOGURT

ABOUT 1 TABLESPOON DIJON-STYLE MUSTARD

ABOUT 1½ TEASPOONS TARRAGON VINEGAR

◆ To make mustard sauce, in a small bowl, mix together mayonnaise and yogurt and stir in mustard and vinegar to taste. Spoon into a small serving bowl and chill lightly.

◆ Place one fish on a board, cut-side down and opened out. Press gently along backbone with your thumbs. Turn fish over and carefully lift away backbone and attached bones.

◆ Season fish with salt and pepper and squeeze lemon juice over both sides, then fold in half, skin-side outwards. Repeat with remaining fish.

◆ Coat fish evenly in oats, pressing in well but gently.

◆ Place herrings on a prepared grill and cook 3 or 4 minutes on each side until brown and crisp and flesh flakes easily. Serve hot with mustard sauce and lemon wedges.

Mediterranean Chargrilled Sardines

MAKES 4 TO 6 SERVINGS

12 SMALL SARDINES

12 SMALL STRIPS LEMON PEEL

12 SMALL ROSEMARY SPRIGS

4 TO 6 LEMON WEDGES, TO SERVE

HERB AND LEMON OIL

¼ CUP EXTRA VIRGIN OLIVE OIL

2 TEASPOONS GRATED LEMON ZEST

JUICE 1 LEMON

1 TABLESPOON CHOPPED FRESH ROSEMARY

1 TABLESPOON CHOPPED FRESH THYME

SALT AND FRESHLY GROUND BLACK PEPPER

◆ Wash sardines and dry on absorbent kitchen paper. Stuff a small strip of lemon peel and a rosemary sprig into the cavity of each sardine.

◆ Thread three sardines onto each pair of skewers by pushing one skewer through a sardine just below the head and pushing the second skewer in just above the tail.

◆ To make herb and lemon oil, mix together in a bowl olive oil, lemon zest and juice, rosemary, thyme, salt, and pepper.

◆ Brush herb and lemon oil liberally over sardines. Cook on a very hot grill 3 or 4 minutes on each side, basting with more oil while they are cooking.

◆ Slide cooked sardines off skewers and serve 2 or 3 to each person, with lemon wedges.

Note: Use a metal fish rack that holds 6 or 12 sardines instead of skewers, if preferred.

Sardines with Caponata

12 LARGE SARDINES

JUICE 1 LEMON

OIL FOR BRUSHING

CAPONATA

6 TABLESPOONS OLIVE OIL

1 ONION, CHOPPED

1 GARLIC CLOVE, CHOPPED

2 CELERY STALKS, SLICED

1 TABLESPOON CHOPPED FRESH BASIL

1 MEDIUM EGGPLANT, DICED

½ CUP PITTED GREEN OLIVES, HALVED

2 TABLESPOONS CAPERS

2 RIPE TOMATOES, CHOPPED

1½ TABLESPOONS RED WINE VINEGAR

1 TEASPOON SUGAR

2 TABLESPOONS PINE NUTS, TOASTED

◆ To make caponata, heat 2 tablespoons oil in a skillet and fry onion, garlic, celery, and basil 5 minutes until browned. Transfer mixture to a bowl with a slotted spoon.

◆ Add remaining oil to pan and fry eggplant 5 or 6 minutes until golden. Add to onion and celery mixture with olives and capers.

◆ Place tomatoes, vinegar, and sugar in a saucepan and bring to a boil. Cover and simmer gently 15 minutes. Stir in vegetable mixture and pine nuts and season to taste. Set aside to cool slightly.

◆ Gradually stir in oil to form a thick sauce. (Thin with 2 or 3 tablespoons boiling water if too thick.) Transfer to a bowl, cover, and set aside.

◆ Brush inside and outside of sardines with oil. Season and squeeze over a little lemon juice. Cook sardines on a prepared grill 4 or 5 minutes on each side until charred and cooked through.

◆ Spoon caponata mixture onto individual serving plates, top each with 2 or 3 sardines, and serve at once.

Mackerel and Gooseberries

MAKES 4 SERVINGS

1 POUND GOOSEBERRIES

1 TEASPOON FENNEL SEEDS

2 MACKEREL, EACH WEIGHING 1 POUND
AND CUT INTO 2 FILLETS

1 TABLESPOON OLIVE OIL

SALT AND FRESHLY GROUND BLACK PEPPER

1 TABLESPOON PASTIS OR OTHER
ANISEED-FLAVORED LIQUEUR

1 TEASPOON SUGAR

2 TABLESPOONS BUTTER, DICED

PARSLEY SPRIGS, TO GARNISH

◆ Put gooseberries and fennel seeds in a saucepan with just enough water to cover. Bring to a boil, then simmer 7 to 10 minutes, until very soft.

◆ With the point of a sharp knife, make three slashes in each mackerel fillet. Season fish, brush with oil on each side, and cook on a prepared grill 10 minutes, turning once.

◆ Reserve a few gooseberries for garnish. Press remainder through a nylon strainer into a saucepan, pressing hard to extract all the juice.

◆ Add pastis, sugar, and salt and pepper and heat gently, gradually beating in butter.

◆ Pour gooseberry sauce over fish, garnish with reserved gooseberries and parsley, and serve.

Mackerel with Mustard

MAKES 4 SERVINGS

2 TABLESPOONS DIJON-STYLE MUSTARD

1/4 CUP FINELY CHOPPED
FRESH CILANTRO

2 GARLIC CLOVES, FINELY CRUSHED

2 OR 3 TEASPOONS LEMON JUICE

SALT AND PEPPER

4 MACKEREL, EACH WEIGHING
ABOUT 10 OUNCES

ROLLED OATS FOR COATING

LEMON WEDGES AND CILANTRO SPRIGS,
TO GARNISH

TOMATO, FENNEL, AND THYME SALAD,
TO SERVE (OPTIONAL)

◆ In a bowl, mix together mustard, cilantro, garlic, and lemon juice and season with salt and pepper.

◆ Using the point of a sharp knife, cut 3 slashes in both sides of each mackerel. Spoon mustard mixture into slashes and sprinkle with a few rolled oats.

◆ Wrap each fish in a large piece of heavy-duty aluminum foil and fold edges of foil together to seal tightly.

◆ Place foil packages on the grill rack over hot coals 5 minutes. Open foil, turn fish, reseal packages, and cook an additional 2 or 3 minutes. Open foil, place fish directly on rack, and cook an additional 2 or 3 minutes until cooked.

◆ Garnish with lemon wedges and cilantro sprigs and serve with tomato, fennel, and thyme salad, if desired.

Sardines with Avgolemono Sauce

MAKES 4 SERVINGS

2¼ POUNDS SARDINES

2 TABLESPOONS COARSE SEA SALT

1 TABLESPOON CHOPPED FRESH OREGANO

1 TABLESPOON CHOPPED FRESH PARSLEY

1 TABLESPOON CHOPPED FRESH FENNEL

LEMON SLICES, TO GARNISH

AVGOLEMONO SAUCE

1¾ CUPS FISH STOCK

SALT AND PEPPER

3 TEASPOONS CORNSTARCH

2 LARGE EGG YOLKS

JUICE 1 LEMON

◆ Slash each sardine twice on each side and sprinkle with sea salt. Put chopped fresh oregano, parsley, and fennel inside cavities of fish. Set aside 30 minutes.

◆ To make avgolemono sauce, put fish stock in a saucepan, season with salt and pepper, and heat. In a bowl, mix cornstarch with a little water. Whisk hot stock into cornstarch mixture and return to pan. Cook gently 10 to 15 minutes, stirring, until sauce thickens.

◆ In a bowl, beat egg yolks. Stir in lemon juice. Add a little hot sauce, then return sauce to pan. Cook gently, without boiling, until thickened.

◆ Place sardines onto rack of prepared grill and cook 1½ or 2 minutes on each side until skins are brown and crisp.

◆ Garnish fish with lemon slices and serve with sauce.

Mackerel with Cucumber Raita

MAKES 4 SERVINGS

1 GARLIC CLOVE, FINELY CRUSHED

½ TEASPOON HARISSA OR
DASH CHILI POWDER

2 TEASPOONS GROUND CUMIN

2 TABLESPOONS LIGHT OLIVE OIL

SQUEEZE LEMON JUICE

SALT AND PEPPER

4 MACKEREL

CUCUMBER RAITA

½ CUCUMBER, PEELED

SALT

¾ CUP PLAIN YOGURT

1¼ TABLESPOONS CHOPPED
FRESH MINT

◆ To make raita, halve cucumber lengthwise, scoop out seeds, and thinly slice flesh. Spread flesh in a colander, sprinkle with salt, and let drain 30 minutes.

◆ Rinse cucumber, dry with absorbent kitchen paper, and mix with yogurt and mint. Cover and chill 2 hours.

◆ Put garlic in a mortar or small bowl, then pound in harissa or chili powder, cumin, and oil, using a pestle or the end of a rolling pin. Add lemon juice and season with salt and pepper.

◆ With the point of a sharp knife, cut 2 slashes in each side of mackerel. Spread spiced oil mixture over fish and leave 15 to 30 minutes.

◆ Cook fish on a prepared grill 7 or 8 minutes on each side. Serve with cucumber raita.

Malaysian Mackerel with Spicy Peanut Sauce

MAKES 6 SERVINGS

¼ CUP SAMBAL OELEK
(HOT PEPPER CONDIMENT)

¼ CUP PEANUT OIL

2 TEASPOONS SOFT BROWN SUGAR

2 GARLIC CLOVES, CRUSHED

JUICE 2 LIMES

6 MEDIUM MACKEREL, EACH WEIGHING
ABOUT 7 OUNCES

SPICY PEANUT SAUCE

1 TABLESPOON TAMARIND CONCENTRATE,
MIXED WITH ½ CUP WATER

4 TEASPOONS SOFT BROWN SUGAR

2 SCALLIONS, CHOPPED

1 LEMON GRASS STALK, CHOPPED

1 GARLIC CLOVE, CRUSHED

1 TABLESPOON SAMBAL OELEK

½ CUP SALTED PEANUTS,
COARSELY GROUND

⅔ CUP COCONUT MILK

◆ In a small bowl mix together sambal oelek, peanut oil, soft brown sugar, garlic, and lime juice.

◆ Make several deep slashes in flesh of each mackerel and place fish in a large shallow dish. Pour over marinade and turn fish to coat well. Cover and refrigerate at least 2 hours.

◆ To make peanut sauce, place tamarind concentrate, soft brown sugar, scallions, lemon grass, garlic, and sambal oelek in a saucepan. Bring to a boil, reduce heat, and simmer 5 minutes.

◆ Add peanuts and cook an additional minute, then stir in coconut milk and simmer an additional 2 minutes. Set aside.

◆ Remove mackerel from marinade, reserving marinade for basting. Cook fish in a wire frame on a prepared grill about 15 minutes, turning and basting fish as they cook.

◆ Serve fish with warm spicy peanut sauce.

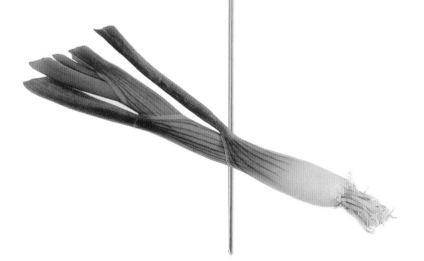

Sardines with Cilantro

MAKES 4 SERVINGS

2¼ POUNDS SARDINES (AT LEAST 12)

¼ CUP OLIVE OIL

GRATED ZEST 1½ LIMES

1½ TABLESPOONS LIME JUICE

¾ TEASPOON FINELY CRUSHED, TOASTED
CORIANDER SEEDS

3 TABLESPOONS CHOPPED FRESH CILANTRO

SALT AND PEPPER

CILANTRO SPRIGS, TO GARNISH

LIME WEDGES, TO SERVE

◆ Put sardines in a shallow, nonmetallic dish. Thoroughly whisk together oil, lime zest and juice, crushed coriander seeds, chopped cilantro, and salt and pepper.

◆ Pour cilantro mixture over sardines and leave 1 hour, turning sardines over once.

◆ Remove sardines from dish and cook on a prepared grill 4 or 5 minutes on each side, basting with cilantro mixture.

◆ Serve sardines garnished with cilantro sprigs and accompanied by lime wedges.

Kabobs

Tandoori Seafood Kabobs

MAKES 4 SERVINGS

2 FLOUNDER, SKINNED AND FILLETED

16 LARGE RAW SHRIMP,
PEELED AND VEINS REMOVED

1 POUND COD FILLET, SKINNED AND DICED

2 LIMES, CUT INTO WEDGES

GREEN SALAD AND NAAN BREAD,
TO SERVE (OPTIONAL)

MARINADE

1 SMALL ONION, VERY FINELY CHOPPED

2 GARLIC CLOVES, CRUSHED

1 TEASPOON GRATED FRESH GINGER

1 TEASPOON MILD CURRY POWDER

1 TEASPOON PAPRIKA

¼ TEASPOON CHILI POWDER

¼ TEASPOON TURMERIC

1 TABLESPOON LEMON JUICE

⅔ CUP PLAIN YOGURT

SALT AND PEPPER

◆ Wash and dry flounder fillets. Cut each one in half lengthwise to make 16 thin strips of fish. Roll up and secure with toothpicks. Place in a shallow dish with shrimp and diced cod.

◆ To make marinade, in a bowl mix together onion, garlic, ginger, curry powder, paprika, chili powder, turmeric, lemon juice, yogurt, and salt and pepper.

◆ Pour marinade over seafood. Cover and marinate 30 minutes.

◆ Meanwhile, soak 8 bamboo skewers in cold water 30 minutes. Drain and pat dry on absorbent kitchen paper.

◆ Thread fish, shrimp, and lime wedges alternately onto bamboo skewers. Place on a preheated grill and cook about 8 minutes, turning and basting, until charred and cooked through.

◆ Place two kabobs on each plate. Serve with a green salad and naan bread and garnish with extra lime wedges, if desired.

Vietnamese Seafood Skewers

12 SCALLOPS

12 LARGE RAW PEELED SHRIMP

8 OUNCES FIRM WHITE FISH FILLET, SUCH AS HALIBUT, COD, OR MONKFISH, CUT INTO 12 CUBES

1 MEDIUM ONION, CUT INTO 12 PIECES

1 RED OR GREEN BELL PEPPER, CUT INTO 12 CUBES

½ CUP DRY WHITE WINE OR SHERRY

1 TABLESPOON CHOPPED DILLWEED

1 TABLESPOON CHOPPED HOLY BASIL LEAVES

1 TABLESPOON LIME JUICE OR VINEGAR

SALT AND FRESHLY GROUND BLACK PEPPER

VEGETABLE OIL FOR BRUSHING

SPICY FISH SAUCE

2 GARLIC CLOVES

2 SMALL FRESH RED OR GREEN CHILIES, SEEDED AND CHOPPED

1 TABLESPOON SUGAR

2 TABLESPOONS LIME JUICE

2 TABLESPOONS FISH SAUCE

◆ To make spicy fish sauce, pound garlic and chilies until finely ground using a mortar and pestle. Place in a bowl and add sugar, lime juice, fish sauce, and 2 or 3 tablespoons water. Blend well and set aside.

◆ In a bowl, mix scallops, shrimp, fish, onion, and red or green bell pepper. In a small bowl or jug, mix together wine or sherry, dill, basil, lime juice or vinegar, salt, and pepper. Pour over seafood and vegetables and let stand in a cool place at least 2 to 3 hours (the longer the better).

◆ Meanwhile, soak 6 bamboo skewers in hot water 25 to 30 minutes.

◆ Thread seafood and vegetables alternately onto skewers so that each skewer has 2 pieces of each ingredient. Brush each filled skewer with a little oil.

◆ Cook skewers on a prepared grill 5 or 6 minutes, turning frequently. Serve hot with fish sauce as a dip.

Mexican Fish Kabobs with Guacamole

1/4 CUP CHOPPED CILANTRO

1/4 CUP OLIVE OIL

JUICE 3 LIMES

4 TEASPOONS PAPRIKA

1 FRESH RED CHILI, SEEDED AND
FINELY CHOPPED

1 1/4 POUNDS RED SNAPPER FILLETS

4 MINI RED BELL PEPPERS, HALVED

2 ONIONS, EACH CUT INTO 8 WEDGES

GUACAMOLE

2 AVOCADOS

JUICE 1 LARGE LIME

1/2 ONION, FINELY CHOPPED

1/3 CUP TORN CILANTRO LEAVES

◆ To make marinade, place chopped cilantro, olive oil, lime juice, paprika, and chopped red chili in a shallow glass bowl and mix well.

◆ Cut fish fillets into chunks, add to marinade, and turn to coat evenly. Cover and refrigerate 2 hours.

◆ To make guacamole, mash avocados with lime juice. Stir in chopped onion and cilantro leaves and season with salt and pepper. Refrigerate until required.

◆ Remove fish from marinade, reserving marinade for basting. Thread fish onto skewers, alternating with bell peppers and onions wedges.

◆ Cook kabobs on a prepared grill about 10 minutes, turning and brushing them with reserved marinade. Serve at once with guacamole.

Scallops with Tindooris

MAKES 6 TO 8 SERVINGS

2 1/4 POUNDS FRESH OR FROZEN SCALLOPS,
THAWED IF FROZEN

12 TINDOORIS

2/3 CUP OLIVE OIL

1 TABLESPOON LEMON JUICE

1 TABLESPOON LIME JUICE

1/4 TEASPOON LEMON PEPPER

1/4 TEASPOON ONION SALT

LEMON AND LIME SLICES, TO GARNISH

◆ Remove and discard any dark veins from scallops. Rinse scallops and pat dry with absorbent kitchen paper.

◆ Rinse tindooris and halve lengthwise. Add to a saucepan of fast-boiling water and cook 1 minute. Drain and let cool.

◆ In a large bowl combine olive oil, lemon and lime juice, lemon pepper, and onion salt. Add scallops and let marinate 1 hour, stirring occasionally. Add tindooris and let marinate an additional 15 minutes.

◆ Thread scallops and tindooris onto oiled skewers and grill on a rack over medium coals 5 to 10 minutes, basting frequently with marinade. Scallops are cooked when opaque.

Monkfish Kabobs with Cherry Tomato Salsa

MAKES 4 SERVINGS

1 SMALL RED ONION, FINELY CHOPPED

1 GARLIC CLOVE, CRUSHED

2 TABLESPOONS CHOPPED FRESH CILANTRO

¼ CUP CHOPPED FRESH PARSLEY

1 TEASPOON GROUND CUMIN

1 TEASPOON PAPRIKA

¼ TEASPOON CHILI POWDER

PINCH SAFFRON THREADS

¼ CUP OLIVE OIL

JUICE 1 LEMON

½ TEASPOON SALT

1½ POUNDS MONKFISH FILLETS, SKINNED

ITALIAN PARSLEY SPRIGS AND CHIVES, TO GARNISH

CHERRY TOMATO SALSA

8 OUNCES RED AND YELLOW CHERRY TOMATOES

1 SMALL RED ONION, THINLY SLICED

1 QUANTITY VINAIGRETTE (SEE PAGE 44)

1 SMALL FRESH GREEN CHILI, SEEDED, AND SLICED

1 TABLESPOON CHOPPED FRESH CHIVES

◆ In a large bowl mix together onion, garlic, cilantro, parsley, cumin, paprika, chili powder, saffron, olive oil, lemon juice, and salt.

◆ Cut monkfish into cubes and add to marinade. Mix well, cover, and let stand in a cool place to marinate 1 hour.

◆ Meanwhile, make cherry tomato salsa. Halve tomatoes and put in a bowl. Add onion, vinaigrette, chili, and chives. Mix well and let stand 30 minutes.

◆ Thread monkfish onto 4 skewers and place on a low rack of a prepared grill. Spoon over a little marinade. Cook 3 minutes on each side until cooked through and lightly browned.

◆ Garnish with parsley sprigs and chives and serve with tomato salsa.

Lime Fish Skewers

MAKES 4 SERVINGS

12 OUNCES MONKFISH TAILS, SKINNED AND CUT INTO ³/₄-INCH CUBES

12 OUNCES TROUT FILLETS, SKINNED AND CUT INTO ³/₄-INCH CUBES

2 LIMES

1 TEASPOON SESAME OIL

LARGE DASH FIVE-SPICE POWDER

FRESHLY GROUND BLACK PEPPER

STRIPS LIME PEEL, TO GARNISH

◆ Place monkfish and trout in a shallow dish. Juice one lime and grate zest. Mix juice and zest with sesame oil and five-spice powder. Pour over fish, cover, and chill 30 minutes.

◆ Soak 4 bamboo skewers in cold water. Halve and quarter remaining lime lengthwise and halve each quarter to make 8 wedges. Slice each piece of lime in half crosswise to make 16 small pieces.

◆ Thread monkfish, trout, and lime pieces onto skewers and place on the rack of a prepared grill. Brush with marinade and season with pepper. Cook 2 minutes on each side, brushing occasionally with marinade to prevent drying out.

◆ Drain on absorbent kitchen paper, then place each kabob on a separate serving plate and garnish with lime zest to serve.

Swordfish Kabobs with Chermoula

MAKES 4 SERVINGS

*1½ POUNDS SKINLESS, BONELESS
SWORDFISH STEAKS*

CHERMOULA

4 GARLIC CLOVES

1 TEASPOON SALT

JUICE 2 LEMONS

1 TABLESPOON GROUND CUMIN

2 TEASPOONS PAPRIKA

*1 FRESH RED CHILI, SEEDED AND
ROUGHLY CHOPPED*

⅓ CUP CHOPPED FRESH CILANTRO

⅓ CUP CHOPPED FRESH PARSLEY

¼ CUP OLIVE OIL

◆ To make chermoula, crush garlic with salt in a mortar and pestle. Place in a blender or food processor.

◆ Add lemon juice to blender or food processor with cumin, paprika, red chile, cilantro, and parsley. Process briefly, then, with the motor running, gradually add olive oil and reduce to a coarse purée. Transfer to a bowl.

◆ Cut swordfish into 1-inch cubes and add to chermoula mixture. Mix well to coat, cover, and let stand in a cool place 1 hour.

◆ Thread fish cubes onto skewers and place on a rack over grill pan. Spoon marinade over fish.

◆ Grill over hot coals 3 to 4 minutes on each side, until fish is lightly browned and flakes easily when tested with a knife.

Variation: Instead of swordfish steaks, try using monkfish or raw tiger shrimp for this recipe.

Shrimp and Monkfish Kabobs with Coconut Salsa

MAKES 6 SERVINGS

18 RAW JUMBO SHRIMP

1 POUND MONKFISH FILLETS

4 LIMES, SLICED

COCONUT SALSA

3 CUPS OLIVE OIL

*2 TEASPOONS SESAME OIL,
PLUS EXTRA FOR BASTING*

*8 SCALLIONS, TRIMMED AND
FINELY CHOPPED*

2 TABLESPOONS CHOPPED FRESH CILANTRO

GRATED ZEST AND JUICE 2 LIMES

1 OR 2 DRIED RED CHILIES, CRUSHED

²/₃ CUP SHREDDED COCONUT

◆ To make salsa, heat olive and sesame oils together in a small pan and sauté scallions and cilantro 2 minutes.

◆ Remove from heat and stir in lime zest and juice, dried red chilies, and shredded coconut. Transfer to a small dish and let cool.

◆ Wash and dry shrimp and, if preferred, remove heads and shells. Cut monkfish into 1-inch pieces.

◆ Thread shrimp, monkfish, and lime slices alternately onto metal skewers and brush all over with sesame oil.

◆ Place skewers on a prepared grill and cook 6 to 8 minutes, turning and basting occasionally, until shrimp and monkfish are lightly charred and cooked through.

◆ Serve at once with coconut salsa.

Scallop Brochettes with Ginger and Orange Butter

Juice 2 oranges

7 teaspoons grated fresh ginger

1/4 cup vegetable oil

4 scallions, finely chopped

2 garlic cloves, crushed

Salt and ground black pepper

16 large scallops

1 stick butter, softened

1 tablespoon grated orange zest

Salt and freshly ground black pepper

4 long strips orange peel

2 medium zucchini, canneled and each cut into 12 chunks

◆ To make marinade, in a large shallow bowl mix together orange juice, reserving 1 tablespoon for butter, 4 teaspoons grated fresh ginger, oil, scallions, garlic, and salt and pepper. Add scallops to marinade and turn to coat evenly. Cover and refrigerate 2 hours.

◆ To make ginger and orange butter, mix together softened butter, remaining ginger and orange juice, orange zest, and salt and pepper. Place butter in a sausage shape on a piece of waxed paper or plastic wrap. Roll up to form a cylinder and refrigerate until butter hardens.

◆ Remove scallops from marinade, reserving marinade for basting. Alternately thread 4 scallops, a strip of orange peel, and 3 chunks of zucchini onto each skewer.

◆ Cook brochettes on a prepared, medium-hot grill 8 to 10 minutes, turning and brushing them frequently with marinade. Serve hot brochettes with discs of flavored butter.

Turmeric Shrimp and Pineapple Skewers

1 lemon grass stalk, finely chopped

1-inch piece fresh ginger, peeled and grated

2 garlic cloves, crushed

2 tablespoons peanut oil

1 tablespoon lemon juice

1 teaspoon turmeric

Dash each sugar, salt and pepper

24 raw tiger shrimp, peeled but with tails left on

8 ounces fresh pineapple

16 bulbous white parts of scallions

◆ Place lemon grass, ginger, garlic, oil, lemon juice, turmeric, sugar, salt, and pepper in a food processor and blend to a paste.

◆ Transfer paste to a large bowl, add shrimp, and turn to coat evenly. Refrigerate 2 to 3 hours or overnight.

◆ Remove shrimp from marinade, reserving marinade for basting. Cut pineapple into 16 chunks and thread onto skewers, alternating with shrimp and scallions.

◆ Cook skewers on a prepared grill 8 to 10 minutes, turning and basting them while they cook. Serve at once.

Swordfish and Cherry Tomato Kabobs

MAKES 4 SERVINGS

Juice 1/2 lemon

1/4 cup olive oil

1 tablespoon chopped fresh fennel

1 tablespoon chopped fresh chives

1 garlic clove, crushed

Salt and pepper

1 pound swordfish fillet

1 small onion

16 cherry tomatoes

Lemon slices and fresh herbs, to garnish

◆ In a bowl mix together lemon juice, oil, fennel, chives, garlic, salt, and pepper. Cut swordfish into ¾-inch cubes. Place in bowl of marinade and let marinate 1 hour.

◆ Cut onion into quarters and separate layers.

◆ Remove fish from marinade, reserving marinade for basting. Thread swordfish, onion, and cherry tomatoes alternately onto 8 skewers.

◆ Place skewers on the rack of a prepared grill and cook 5 to 10 minutes, turning occasionally and basting with reserved marinade.

◆ Serve kabobs garnished with lemon slices and herb sprigs.

Turkish Swordfish Kabobs

MAKES 4 SERVINGS

¼ CUP LEMON JUICE

¼ CUP OLIVE OIL

1 SHALLOT, FINELY CHOPPED

3 FRESH BAY LEAVES, TORN

1½ TEASPOONS PAPRIKA

SALT AND PEPPER

*1¼ POUNDS SWORDFISH, CUT INTO
1 x 1½-INCH CUBES*

PARSLEY SPRIGS, TO GARNISH

LEMON SAUCE

3 TABLESPOONS OLIVE OIL

3 TABLESPOONS LEMON JUICE

3 TABLESPOONS CHOPPED FRESH PARSLEY

SALT AND PEPPER

◆ To prepare marinade, mix together lemon juice, olive oil, shallot, bay leaves, paprika, salt, and pepper.

◆ Lay swordfish in a single layer in a wide, shallow, nonmetallic dish. Pour over marinade, turn fish so it is evenly coated, then cover and let marinate in a cool place 4 to 5 hours, turning fish occasionally.

◆ To make lemon sauce, mix together olive oil, lemon juice, and chopped parsley and season with salt and pepper. Set aside.

◆ Remove fish from marinade and thread onto 4 skewers. Grill 4 or 5 minutes on each side, basting frequently.

◆ Serve kabobs with sauce, garnished with parsley sprigs.

Swordfish Kabobs with Puy Lentils

⅔ CUP PUY LENTILS, SOAKED

½ CUP OLIVE OIL

1 RED ONION, DICED

1 SMALL RED BELL PEPPER, SEEDED AND DICED

1 GARLIC CLOVE, CRUSHED

JUICE 1 LEMON

2 TABLESPOONS CHOPPED FRESH BASIL

½ CUP PITTED BLACK OLIVES, CHOPPED

1½ POUNDS SWORDFISH STEAK, DICED

◆ Drain lentils well, place in a pan, and cover with cold water. Bring to a boil, then simmer gently 35 to 40 minutes until tender. Drain.

◆ Heat 2 tablespoons olive oil in a skillet and fry onion, bell pepper, and garlic 5 minutes. Add lemon juice, lentils, basil, and olives and simmer gently 3 minutes. Keep warm.

◆ Thread cubed swordfish onto 8 small skewers. Brush with a little remaining oil and place on the rack of a prepared grill. Cook 4 or 5 minutes, turning and basting, until golden and firm to the touch.

◆ Stir remaining oil into lentil mixture and heat through. Spoon onto warmed plates and top with kabobs. Serve at once.

Tuna Fish Saté

MAKES 6 SERVINGS

2 POUNDS FRESH TUNA STEAKS

3 TABLESPOONS LIGHT SOY SAUCE

1 TABLESPOON SESAME OIL

1 TABLESPOON CLEAR HONEY

1 TABLESPOON DRY SHERRY

JUICE 1 LIME

1 GARLIC CLOVE, CRUSHED

1-INCH PIECE FRESH GINGER, GRATED

SATÉ SAUCE

¼ CUP RAW PEANUTS, GROUND

JUICE 1 LIME

⅓ CUP GRATED CREAMED COCONUT

¼ TEASPOON CAYENNE

DASH SUGAR

◆ Wash and dry tuna and cut into ½-inch cubes. Place in a large shallow dish.

◆ To make marinade, blend together soy sauce, sesame oil, honey, sherry, lime juice, garlic, grated ginger, and 2 tablespoons water. Pour over fish. Cover and leave 1 to 2 hours, turning fish occasionally.

◆ Drain and reserve marinade and thread 6 cubes of tuna onto each skewer. Cover and keep cool.

◆ To make sauce, put 6 tablespoons reserved marinade into a small pan and bring to a boil. Stir in ground peanuts, lime juice, creamed coconut, cayenne, a dash of sugar, and 2 tablespoons water.

◆ Simmer sauce over a low heat until slightly thickened. Transfer to a small bowl and let cool.

◆ Cook tuna saté over a hot grill 5 or 6 minutes, turning frequently and basting with remaining marinade until cooked. Serve with sauce.

Seafood Brochettes with Saffron Sauce

MAKES 4 SERVINGS

12 OUNCES SKINLESS, BONELESS
SALMON STEAK

12 OUNCES SKINLESS, BONELESS
MONKFISH

16 LARGE RAW SHRIMP

1/4 CUP SUNFLOWER OIL

1/2 CUP CHOPPED FRESH CHERVIL

SAFFRON SAUCE

1 TABLESPOON SUNFLOWER OIL

2 SHALLOTS, FINELY CHOPPED

2 1/2 CUPS DRY WHITE WINE

1/2 TEASPOON SAFFRON THREADS, SOAKED
IN 2 TABLESPOONS BOILING WATER

1 1/4 CUPS LIGHT CREAM

2 TABLESPOONS CHOPPED FRESH CHERVIL

2 TABLESPOONS CHOPPED FRESH CHIVES

◆ Cut salmon and monkfish into 16 chunks each. Place fish and shrimp in a shallow glass dish.

◆ To make marinade, mix sunflower oil with chopped chervil and season with salt and pepper. Pour over seafood and toss to coat evenly. Cover and refrigerate 2 hours.

◆ To make saffron sauce, heat oil in a saucepan and sauté shallots 3 minutes. Add wine and saffron with water, bring to a boil, and boil steadily 10 to 12 minutes, until liquid has reduced to about one quarter of its original amount.

◆ Add cream and reduce again 4 or 5 minutes. Add chervil, chives, and seasoning and heat an additional 30 seconds. Set aside.

◆ Remove fish and shrimp from marinade, reserving marinade for basting, and divide them equally between 8 skewers. Cook on oiled rack of a prepared grill 8 to 10 minutes, turning and brushing with marinade.

◆ Reheat sauce and serve it at once with brochettes.

Seared Scallop and Rosemary Kabobs

SERVES 8 AS AN APPETIZER

1/4 CUP WALNUT OIL

2 TABLESPOONS SHERRY VINEGAR

1 SMALL BUNCH BASIL

1/2 CUP SUN-DRIED TOMATOES IN OIL,
DRAINED AND FINELY CHOPPED

FRESHLY GROUND BLACK PEPPER

48 BAY OR SMALL SCALLOPS

16 ROSEMARY SPRIGS

ARUGULA LEAVES, TO SERVE

◆ To make marinade, whisk together walnut oil and sherry vinegar. Chop basil leaves and discard stems. Stir basil into oil and vinegar with sun-dried tomatoes. Season with black pepper. Set aside.

◆ Thread 3 scallops onto each rosemary sprig. Place in a shallow dish, pour dressing over, and turn scallops to coat in dressing. Let marinate in a cool place 30 minutes.

◆ Remove scallop kabobs from marinade and cook on the grill over hot coals about 2 minutes, turning and basting with remaining marinade.

◆ Serve on a bed of arugula leaves.

Malaysian Shrimp Balls

SERVES 8 AS AN APPETIZER

1½ POUNDS LARGE RAW UNPEELED SHRIMP

1 GARLIC CLOVE, CHOPPED

1½ TABLESPOONS FISH SAUCE

½ TEASPOON LIGHT BROWN SUGAR

2 TEASPOONS PEANUT OIL

1 TABLESPOON CORNSTARCH

1 EGG, BEATEN

SALT AND FRESHLY GROUND BLACK PEPPER

½ CUP SHREDDED COCONUT

2 TABLESPOONS DRIED BREADCRUMBS

CILANTRO SPRIGS, TO GARNISH

DIPPING SAUCE

1 GARLIC CLOVE, MASHED WITH SMALL DASH SALT

¼ CUP LIGHT SOY SAUCE

2½ TABLESPOONS LIME JUICE

1 TABLESPOON VERY FINELY SLICED SCALLION

1 TEASPOON LIGHT BROWN SUGAR

1 OR 2 DROPS CHILI SAUCE

◆ Reserve 8 shrimp in their shells and peel remainder. With the point of a sharp knife, cut a slit along the back of each peeled shrimp. Remove and discard black intestinal thread.

◆ Put shrimp in a food processor with garlic, fish sauce, sugar, oil, cornstarch, egg, salt, and pepper. Mix to a smooth purée. Transfer to a bowl, cover, and chill 1½ hours.

◆ Meanwhile, make dipping sauce. Mix garlic, soy sauce, lime juice, scallion, and sugar in a small bowl and add chili sauce to taste.

◆ On a baking sheet, combine coconut and breadcrumbs. Wet the palms of your hands and roll shrimp mixture into 1-inch diameter balls. Coat balls in coconut mixture.

◆ Thread shrimp balls onto oiled, long metal skewers, adding a reserved shrimp to each skewer. Cook on a prepared grill, turning occasionally, about 6 minutes, until shrimp balls are firm and whole shrimp have turned pink.

◆ Garnish with cilantro sprigs and serve with dipping sauce.

Squid and Shrimp Kabobs with Garlic Mayonnaise

SERVES 4 AS AN APPETIZER

JUICE 1/2 LEMON

2 TEASPOONS CLEAR HONEY

2 TABLESPOONS OLIVE OIL

12 OUNCES CLEANED SQUID,
CUT INTO 1/4-INCH RINGS

8 LARGE RAW PEELED SHRIMP

SALT AND PEPPER

LEMON SLICES AND CHOPPED FRESH
PARSLEY, TO GARNISH

GARLIC MAYONNAISE

4 GARLIC CLOVES

2 EGG YOLKS

1 1/4 CUPS OLIVE OIL

JUICE 1/2 LEMON

◆ To make marinade, mix together lemon juice, honey, and olive oil in a bowl. Add squid, cover, and let marinate in a cool place 6 hours.

◆ To make mayonnaise, crush garlic to a smooth pulp using a mortar and pestle. Put garlic in a blender or food processor with egg yolks and a little salt.

◆ With the motor running, gradually pour in half the oil. When mixture begins to thicken, add lemon juice and pepper. Add remaining oil.

◆ Drain squid and pat dry with absorbent kitchen paper. Thread onto wooden skewers, alternating with shrimp. Season with salt and pepper.

◆ Cook kabobs on the grill 4 or 5 minutes, turning occasionally, until golden.

◆ Cut lemon slices in half and dip cut edges in chopped parsley. Garnish kabobs with lemon slices and serve with garlic mayonnaise.

Skewered Tuna Rolls

1½ POUNDS FRESH TUNA,
SLICED ¼-INCH THICK

1 TABLESPOON CHOPPED FRESH SAGE

1 TABLESPOON CHOPPED FRESH ROSEMARY

2 DRIED BAY LEAVES, CRUMBLED

1 TEASPOON DRIED CHILI FLAKES

SALT AND FRESHLY GROUND BLACK PEPPER

12 FRESH BAY LEAVES

2 LEMONS, EACH CUT INTO 6 WEDGES

1 TABLESPOON OLIVE OIL

1 TABLESPOON LEMON JUICE

◆ Soak 4 bamboo skewers in cold water 30 minutes.

◆ Meanwhile, place tuna slices between sheets of plastic wrap and beat gently with a rolling pin until thin.

◆ Mix sage, rosemary, dried bay leaves, and chili flakes together. Sprinkle mixture over tuna slices and season with salt and pepper.

◆ Roll up each slice of tuna neatly. Thread onto bamboo skewers, alternately with fresh bay leaves and lemon wedges. Brush with olive oil and lemon juice, mixed together.

◆ Grill 2 or 3 minutes on each side until just cooked.

Seafood

Spicy Jumbo Shrimp with Guacamole

SERVES 6 AS AN APPETIZER

2 GARLIC CLOVES, CRUSHED

1 SMALL BUNCH CILANTRO, FINELY CHOPPED

JUICE 2 LIMES

1 FRESH RED CHILI, SEEDED AND FINELY CHOPPED

5 TABLESPOONS SUNFLOWER OIL

24 LARGE RAW SHRIMP, PEELED, BUT WITH TAILS LEFT ON

GUACAMOLE

1 GARLIC CLOVE, CRUSHED

4 TOMATOES, PEELED AND FINELY CHOPPED

1 FRESH GREEN CHILI, SEEDED AND FINELY CHOPPED

JUICE 1 LIME

2 TABLESPOONS CHOPPED FRESH CILANTRO

SALT AND FRESHLY GROUND BLACK PEPPER

1 LARGE RIPE AVOCADO

◆ In a shallow nonmetallic dish, mix together garlic, cilantro, lime juice, chili, and sunflower oil. Add shrimp and mix well. Cover and chill 1 to 2 hours, turning occasionally.

◆ To make guacamole, put garlic, tomatoes, chili, lime juice, cilantro, and salt and pepper in a bowl and mix well.

◆ Halve avocado lengthwise and remove pit. Using a teaspoon, scoop out flesh, taking care to scrape away dark green flesh closest to skin. Mash into tomato mixture.

◆ Remove shrimp from marinade and arrange on grill rack. Cook 2 or 3 minutes on each side, basting with marinade. Serve with guacamole.

Note: Don't prepare guacamole more than 30 minutes before serving or avocado will discolor.

Grilled Shrimp on Rice Vermicelli

MAKES 4 SERVINGS

VEGETABLE OIL FOR DEEP-FRYING

4 OUNCES RICE VERMICELLI

1 POUND RAW UNPEELED SHRIMP, HEADS REMOVED

2 TEASPOONS VEGETABLE OIL

2 OR 3 SCALLIONS, CHOPPED

2 OR 3 SMALL FRESH RED CHILIES, CHOPPED

1 TABLESPOON ROASTED PEANUTS, CRUSHED, TO GARNISH

CILANTRO SPRIGS, TO GARNISH

SPICY FISH SAUCE (SEE PAGE 59), TO SERVE

◆ Heat oil for deep-frying to 300F. Break vermicelli into short strands and deep-fry, a handful at a time, about 30 seconds, or until strands puff up and turn white. Remove vermicelli and drain, then place on a warm serving dish or plate.

◆ Cook shrimp on the grill rack over hot coals about 3 or 4 minutes. When cooked, arrange on bed of crispy rice vermicelli.

◆ Heat 2 teaspoons oil in a small saucepan until hot, removing from heat before it starts to smoke, and steep scallions and chilies a few minutes. Pour mixture all over shrimp.

◆ Garnish with crushed peanuts and cilantro sprigs and serve with spicy fish sauce as a dip.

Lobster with Fennel Sauce

MAKES 2 SERVINGS

*2 RAW LOBSTERS,
EACH WEIGHING ABOUT 1 POUND*

⅓ CUP OLIVE OIL

2 GARLIC CLOVES, CRUSHED

1 TABLESPOON CHOPPED FENNEL FRONDS

1 TEASPOON DRIED OREGANO

FENNEL SAUCE

½ CUP OLIVE OIL

JUICE 1 LEMON

1 GARLIC CLOVE, CRUSHED

2 TABLESPOONS CHOPPED FENNEL FRONDS

1 TABLESPOON CHOPPED FRESH PARSLEY

◆ Cut lobsters in half through the center of their heads and bodies. Arrange cut-side up in a shallow dish.

◆ To make marinade, combine olive oil, garlic, fennel fronds, and dried oregano in a bowl. Pour marinade over lobsters, cover, and let marinate 1 hour.

◆ To make fennel sauce, place oil in a bowl and gradually whisk in ¼ cup boiling water. Add lemon juice, garlic, and chopped fennel and parsley. Continue to whisk 1 minute until sauce is slightly thickened.

◆ Remove lobsters from marinade and place cut-side down on the grill rack. Cook 8 to 10 minutes, until flesh has become opaque and shells have turned orange.

◆ Serve hot with fennel sauce.

Luxury Ginger Scampi

MAKES 4 SERVINGS

⅔ CUP SALAD OIL

GRATED ZEST AND JUICE 1 SMALL LEMON

⅓ CUP SOY SAUCE

1 GARLIC CLOVE, CRUSHED

1 TEASPOON FINELY GRATED FRESH GINGER

½ TEASPOON DRIED MARJORAM

*1½ POUNDS RAW DUBLIN BAY SHRIMP TAILS
(SEE NOTE)*

*MARJORAM SPRIGS AND LEMON SLICES,
TO GARNISH*

◆ To make marinade, mix together salad oil, lemon juice and zest, soy sauce, garlic, ginger, and dried marjoram in a large bowl.

◆ Wash shrimp but leave shells intact if using unpeeled shrimp tails. Add to bowl of marinade and turn to coat. Leave in a cool place 2 hours, basting occasionally.

◆ Thread shrimp tails crosswise onto skewers and grill over hot coals 7 to 10 minutes, turning frequently until shrimp are opaque.

◆ Remove from skewers and serve at once, garnished with marjoram sprigs and lemon slices.

Note: Frozen, peeled raw shrimp tails may be easier to obtain. These should be thawed before grilling.

Scallops with Arugula Pesto

MAKES 4 SERVINGS

16 SHELLED SCALLOPS

OLIVE OIL FOR BRUSHING

SALT AND FRESHLY GROUND BLACK PEPPER

*LEMON WEDGES AND ARUGULA LEAVES,
TO GARNISH*

ARUGULA PESTO

1 CUP ARUGULA

¼ CUP PINE NUTS

2 GARLIC CLOVES, CRUSHED

½ CUP GRATED PARMESAN CHEESE

JUICE ½ LEMON

⅔ CUP OLIVE OIL

Note: Double skewers are best for holding scallops in place on the grill.

◆ To make arugula pesto, put arugula, pine nuts, garlic, Parmesan cheese, and lemon juice in a food processor or blender and process until well blended.

◆ With the motor running, gradually pour in olive oil until combined. Season with salt and pepper. Transfer to a serving dish and set aside.

◆ Cut each scallop in half and thread scallops onto 8 pairs of skewers. Brush scallops with olive oil and season with salt.

◆ Place skewers on prepared grill and cook 1 minute. Turn and cook an additional minute until browned on the outside but still moist in the center.

◆ Garnish with lemon wedges and arugula leaves and serve with arugula pesto.

Spanish-style Shrimp

MAKES 4 SERVINGS

*1 POUND RAW JUMBO SHRIMP, PEELED
BUT WITH TAILS LEFT ON*

5 TABLESPOONS EXTRA VIRGIN OLIVE OIL

½ GARLIC CLOVE, FINELY CRUSHED

JUICE 1 LEMON

SALT AND FRESHLY GROUND BLACK PEPPER

*1 LARGE TOMATO, PEELED,
SEEDED, AND FINELY CHOPPED*

½ SMALL RED CHILI, SEEDED AND CHOPPED

1 TABLESPOON CHOPPED FRESH PARSLEY

*PARSLEY SPRIGS AND LEMON SLICES
AND ZEST, TO GARNISH*

◆ Using a small sharp knife, make a fine cut along spine of each shrimp and remove black vein.

◆ Thread shrimp onto small skewers and place in a shallow dish.

◆ In a small bowl, stir together 2 tablespoons oil, garlic, 1½ tablespoons lemon juice, and salt and pepper. Pour over shrimp and leave 30 minutes.

◆ Lift shrimp from dish and place on grill rack of prepared grill. Brush with any remaining marinade and grill 3 to 4 minutes until bright pink.

◆ In another small bowl, stir together remaining oil and lemon juice, tomato, chili, parsley, and salt and pepper. Spoon over hot shrimp.

◆ Serve garnished with parsley sprigs and lemon slices and zest.

Crumbed Oysters with Piquant Tomato Dip

SERVES 4 AS AN APPETIZER

½ STICK BUTTER

⅔ CUP FRESH WHITE BREADCRUMBS

2 SCALLIONS, FINELY CHOPPED

1 TABLESPOON CHOPPED FRESH THYME

GENEROUS DASH PAPRIKA

SALT AND FRESHLY GROUND BLACK PEPPER

16 FRESH OYSTERS

PIQUANT TOMATO DIP

5 MEDIUM TOMATOES, ROUGHLY CHOPPED

4 SCALLIONS, FINELY CHOPPED

4 TEASPOONS HORSERADISH SAUCE

2 TEASPOONS WORCESTERSHIRE SAUCE

FEW DROPS TABASCO SAUCE

1 TEASPOON SUGAR

SALT AND FRESHLY GROUND BLACK PEPPER

◆ Prepare tomato dip. Place tomatoes in a food processor and blend briefly to produce a thick purée.

◆ Transfer tomatoes to a saucepan, add scallions, horseradish, Worcestershire and Tabasco sauces, sugar, salt, and pepper and bring to a boil.

◆ Boil sauce steadily about 10 minutes until thick. Taste and adjust seasoning, if necessary, and set aside.

◆ Melt butter in a skillet, add breadcrumbs, and cook 1 minute. Stir in scallions, thyme, paprika, and salt and pepper.

◆ Open oysters, leaving them on the half shell. Top each oyster with a little crispy breadcrumb mixture, making sure coating covers oysters.

◆ Cook oysters on a prepared grill 4 or 5 minutes, until lightly cooked and heated through.

◆ Reheat tomato dip and serve with oysters.

Crab-stuffed Fishcakes

MAKES 6 TO 8 SERVINGS

1½ POUNDS MINCED WHITE FISH

1 SMALL ONION, VERY FINELY CHOPPED

ABOUT ½ CUP MEDIUM MATZO MEAL

1 TABLESPOON GROUND ALMONDS

SALT AND PEPPER

3 EGGS

4 OUNCES MIXED WHITE AND BROWN CRAB MEAT

SUNFLOWER OIL FOR BRUSHING

◆ In a small bowl, beat 2 eggs. In another bowl, combine fish, onion, ¼ cup matzo meal, ground almonds, salt, and pepper. Bind mixture with beaten egg, adding more matzo meal if necessary to form a mixture that holds together when shaped.

◆ Divide mixture into 16 portions, shape into balls, and flatten with the palm of the hand on a work surface sprinkled with matzo meal.

◆ Place a teaspoon of crab meat in the centers and wrap minced fish around to reform into balls. Press down lightly to make fishcake shapes.

◆ Beat remaining egg in a bowl and sprinkle remaining matzo meal onto a plate. Dip fishcakes in beaten egg, then in matzo meal.

◆ Brush both sides of each fishcake with sunflower oil and cook on a grill rack over hot coals 6 to 8 minutes on each side.

Chargrilled Lobster with Herb Butter

MAKES 2 SERVINGS

2 RAW LOBSTERS, EACH WEIGHING ABOUT 1 POUND, SPLIT IN HALF LENGTHWISE WITH CLAWS CRACKED

SALT AND GROUND BLACK PEPPER

HERB BUTTER

3 TABLESPOONS BUTTER, SOFTENED

1 TABLESPOON CHOPPED FRESH CHERVIL

1 TEASPOON CHOPPED FRESH CHIVES

1 TEASPOON FINELY CHOPPED SHALLOT

SQUEEZE LEMON JUICE

SALT AND GROUND BLACK PEPPER

◆ To make herb butter, put butter, chervil, chives, shallot, lemon juice, salt, and pepper into a bowl and beat together to combine.

◆ Place flavored butter in a sausage shape on a piece of waxed paper or plastic wrap. Roll up to produce a cylinder and refrigerate to harden.

◆ Season lobster flesh lightly with salt and pepper and cook lobster halves, cut-side down, on a prepared grill 8 to 10 minutes, until flesh has become opaque and shells have turned orange.

◆ Serve freshly grilled lobster with discs of herb butter.

Tiger Shrimp with Cilantro Mayonnaise

MAKES 2 SERVINGS

¼ CUP SWEET CHILI SAUCE

¼ CUP TOMATO PASTE

4 TEASPOONS LEMON JUICE

4 GARLIC CLOVES, CRUSHED

4 TEASPOONS SESAME OIL

16 RAW UNPEELED TIGER SHRIMP

CILANTRO MAYONNAISE

⅓ CUP MAYONNAISE

½ FRESH RED CHILI, SEEDED AND FINELY CHOPPED

½ SMALL RED ONION, FINELY CHOPPED

2 TABLESPOONS CHOPPED CILANTRO

2 TABLESPOONS LEMON JUICE

◆ To make marinade, combine sweet chili sauce, tomato paste, lemon juice, garlic, and sesame oil in a large bowl.

◆ Add shrimp to bowl of marinade and toss to coat evenly. Cover and refrigerate 2 hours, if time permits.

◆ To make cilantro mayonnaise, mix together mayonnaise, chili, onion, cilantro, and lemon juice. Season to taste with salt and pepper. Cover and refrigerate until required.

◆ Thread 4 shrimp onto each skewer and cook on a prepared grill 4 or 5 minutes on each side, turning them once.

◆ Serve shrimp hot, on or off skewers, with cilantro mayonnaise.

Shrimp with Saffron Mayonnaise

MAKES 4 SERVINGS

3 TABLESPOONS OLIVE OIL

JUICE ½ LEMON

2 GARLIC CLOVES, CRUSHED

1 TABLESPOON CHOPPED FRESH FENNEL

SALT AND FRESHLY GROUND BLACK PEPPER

20 LARGE RAW SHRIMP, HEADS REMOVED

RADICCHIO LEAVES AND FENNEL SPRIGS,
TO GARNISH (OPTIONAL)

SAFFRON MAYONNAISE

⅔ CUP FISH STOCK

GENEROUS PINCH SAFFRON THREADS

⅔ CUP MAYONNAISE

1 TEASPOON LEMON JUICE

◆ To make marinade, mix together oil, lemon juice, garlic, fennel, salt, and pepper.

◆ Put shrimp in a shallow dish and pour marinade over. Turn to coat and chill 2 hours.

◆ To make saffron mayonnaise, put fish stock in a saucepan and boil until reduced to 1 tablespoon. Add saffron threads and let cool.

◆ Strain stock into a bowl and stir in mayonnaise. Stir in lemon juice, salt, and pepper.

◆ Remove shrimp from marinade and thread onto skewers. Cook on a prepared grill about 10 minutes, turning once.

◆ Remove shrimp from skewers and arrange on serving plates. Garnish with radicchio leaves and fennel, if desired, and serve with saffron mayonnaise.

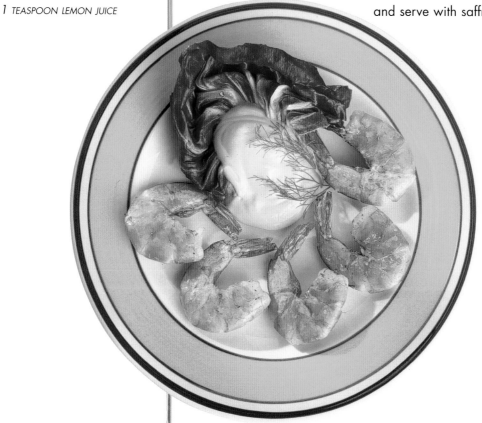

Shrimp with Mango Salsa

MAKES 4 SERVINGS

*1 FRESH RED CHILI, SEEDED AND
FINELY CHOPPED*

1/2 TEASPOON PAPRIKA

1/2 TEASPOON GROUND CORIANDER

1 GARLIC CLOVE, CRUSHED

JUICE 1/2 LIME

2 TABLESPOONS OIL

SALT AND FRESHLY GROUND BLACK PEPPER

20 LARGE RAW UNPEELED SHRIMP

MANGO SALSA

1 MANGO, PEELED AND DICED

1/2 SMALL RED ONION, FINELY DICED

*1 FRESH RED CHILI, SEEDED AND
FINELY CHOPPED*

3 TABLESPOONS CHOPPED FRESH CILANTRO

GRATED ZEST AND JUICE 1 LIME

SALT AND FRESHLY GROUND BLACK PEPPER

◆ To make salsa, in a bowl mix together mango, red onion, chili, cilantro, lime zest and juice and salt and pepper. Set aside.

◆ In a bowl, mix together chili, paprika, cilantro, garlic, lime juice, oil, and salt, and pepper.

◆ Remove dark veins and heads from shrimp and discard. Place shrimp in a dish, add spice mixture, and mix to coat thoroughly. Cover and leave in a cool place 30 minutes.

◆ Thread shrimp onto skewers and cook on a prepared grill 6 to 8 minutes until pink, basting and turning frequently.

◆ Serve shrimp with mango salsa.

Shrimp with Asian-style Sauce

MAKES 4 TO 6 SERVINGS

*HANDFUL THAI OR ORDINARY FRESH BASIL,
FINELY CHOPPED*

2 TABLESPOONS FINELY CHOPPED GARLIC

*2 TABLESPOONS FINELY CHOPPED
FRESH GINGER*

*2 TABLESPOONS FINELY CHOPPED
FRESH GREEN CHILIES*

*2 TEASPOONS RICE WINE OR
MEDIUM-DRY SHERRY*

2½ TABLESPOONS PEANUT OIL

1 TEASPOON CHINESE SESAME OIL

SALT AND PEPPER

1½ POUNDS LARGE RAW SHRIMP

*LIME WEDGES AND BASIL SPRIGS,
TO GARNISH*

◆ To make marinade, pound together basil, garlic, ginger, chilies, rice wine or sherry, peanut and sesame oils, and seasoning using a mortar and pestle.

◆ Remove legs and heads from shrimp and discard. Using strong scissors, cut shrimp lengthwise in half leaving tails intact. Remove dark veins.

◆ Rub marinade over shrimp and place in a bowl. Cover and leave in a cool place 1 hour.

◆ Cook shrimp in a single layer on a prepared grill about 3 minutes until curled, or "butterflied", and bright pink.

◆ Garnish with lime wedges and basil sprigs. Serve any remaining marinade separately.

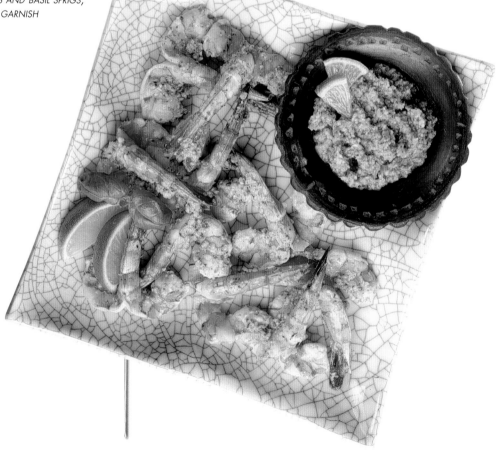

Shrimp with Sun-dried Tomato and Basil Dip

MAKES 4 SERVINGS

1 POUND LARGE RAW SHRIMP

JUICE 1 LEMON

5 TABLESPOONS EXTRA VIRGIN OLIVE OIL

½ GARLIC CLOVE, CRUSHED

2 TABLESPOONS SUN-DRIED TOMATO PASTE

DASH CAYENNE

1 TABLESPOON CHOPPED FRESH BASIL

SALT AND FRESHLY GROUND BLACK PEPPER

FRESH BASIL LEAVES, TO GARNISH

◆ Remove heads and legs from shrimp. Using sharp scissors cut shrimp lengthwise almost in half, leaving tail end intact.

◆ Place shrimp in a shallow dish and pour over half the lemon juice and 2 tablespoons olive oil. Stir in garlic. Let marinate at least 30 minutes.

◆ Remove shrimp from marinade and arrange in a single layer on the grill rack. Cook over hot coals about 3 minutes until shrimp have curled, or "butterflied", and are bright pink.

◆ In a small bowl, mix together remaining lemon juice and 3 tablespoons olive oil, sun-dried tomato paste, cayenne, basil, salt, and pepper.

◆ Either spoon sauce over shrimp or serve separately for dipping. Garnish shrimp with basil sprigs.

Stuffed Squid with Sesame and Cashews

MAKES 4 SERVINGS

12 PREPARED BABY SQUID TUBES

2 TABLESPOONS CORNSTARCH, STRAINED

2 EGG WHITES, BEATEN

2 TEASPOONS LIGHT SOY SAUCE

1 TEASPOON SESAME OIL

*1¼ CUPS RAW CASHEWS,
FINELY CHOPPED*

¼ CUP SESAME SEEDS

THAI SWEET CHILI SAUCE, TO SERVE

*SHREDDED SCALLION AND CUCUMBER,
TO SERVE*

STUFFING

5 CUPS COOKED WHITE RICE

4 SCALLIONS, FINELY CHOPPED

*2 TEASPOONS FINELY CHOPPED
FRESH GINGER*

*1 TEASPOON FINELY CHOPPED
FRESH RED CHILI*

2 TEASPOONS LIGHT SOY SAUCE

◆ To make stuffing, place cooked rice, scallions, ginger, chili, and soy sauce in a food processor and blend briefly until well combined. Stuff cavities of squid with rice mixture.

◆ In a small bowl, mix together cornstarch, egg whites, soy sauce, and sesame oil.

◆ Mix chopped cashews and sesame seeds together and spread out on a plate.

◆ Dip each stuffed squid tube in egg mixture and then roll in cashew and sesame mixture to coat evenly.

◆ Secure end of each squid tube with a toothpick to hold in stuffing. Chill coated squid in refrigerator 2 hours.

◆ Oil a griddle and heat it on a prepared grill. Cook squid on griddle about 8 minutes, turning occasionally until golden.

◆ Serve squid hot with chili sauce and shredded scallion and cucumber.

Angels on Horseback

SERVES 4 AS AN APPETIZER

4 BACON SLICES, RINDS REMOVED

8 SHELLED OYSTERS

4 SLICES BREAD

UNSALTED BUTTER FOR SPREADING

FRESHLY GROUND BLACK PEPPER

CORN SALAD AND LEMON TWISTS, TO GARNISH

◆ Cut each bacon slice crosswise in half, then stretch each piece.

◆ Wrap a piece of bacon around each oyster and place on the rack of a prepared grill, tucking ends of bacon underneath. Cook until just crisp on both sides.

◆ Toast bread, then cut 2 circles from each slice of toast using a pastry cutter. Butter circles.

◆ Place an oyster on each toast circle, grind over black pepper, and serve garnished with corn salad and lemon twists.

Shrimp Paste on Sugar Cane

SERVES 4 AS AN APPETIZER

14 OUNCES RAW PEELED SHRIMP

2 OUNCES FRESH FATTY PORK, CHOPPED

½ TEASPOON CHOPPED GARLIC

SALT AND FRESHLY GROUND BLACK PEPPER

1 TEASPOON SUGAR

1 TABLESPOON CORNSTARCH

1 EGG WHITE, BEATEN

12-INCH PIECE SUGAR CANE

CILANTRO SPRIGS, TO GARNISH

SPICY FISH SAUCE (SEE PAGE 59), TO SERVE

◆ Using a mortar and pestle, pound shrimp, pork, and garlic to a smooth paste. Place in a bowl and add salt, pepper, sugar, cornstarch, and beaten egg white. Mix to blend well.

◆ Peel sugar cane, cut into 3 equal pieces, and split lengthwise into 4.

◆ Mould shrimp paste onto sugar cane, leaving about 1 inch of sugar cane at one end uncovered, to use as a handle.

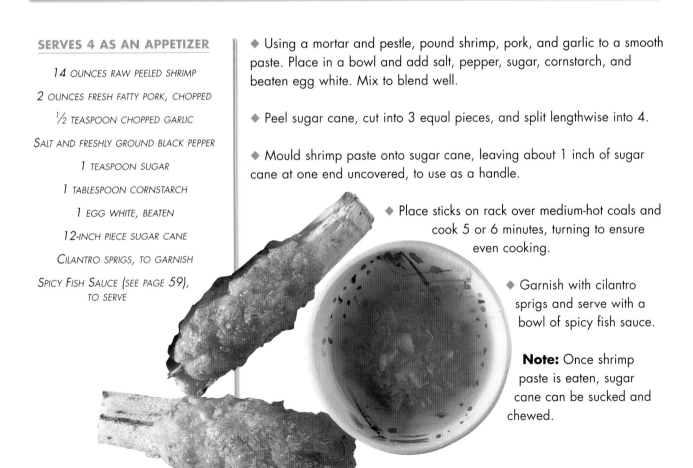

◆ Place sticks on rack over medium-hot coals and cook 5 or 6 minutes, turning to ensure even cooking.

◆ Garnish with cilantro sprigs and serve with a bowl of spicy fish sauce.

Note: Once shrimp paste is eaten, sugar cane can be sucked and chewed.

Shrimp with Ginger Dip

MAKES 4 SERVINGS

*16 LARGE RAW SHRIMP, PEELED BUT WITH
TAILS LEFT ON*

1 TABLESPOON LIGHT SOY SAUCE

1 TEASPOON RICE WINE

1 TEASPOON SESAME OIL

1 GARLIC CLOVE, CRUSHED

*CILANTRO LEAVES AND GINGER STRIPS,
TO GARNISH*

GINGER DIP

1 TABLESPOON WHITE RICE VINEGAR

1 TEASPOON SUGAR

2 TABLESPOONS CHOPPED FRESH CILANTRO

*½-INCH PIECE FRESH GINGER,
PEELED AND FINELY CHOPPED*

◆ Using a small sharp knife, cut along back of each shrimp and remove and discard thin black vein. Rinse and dry shrimp with absorbent kitchen paper and place on a plate.

◆ To make marinade, mix together soy sauce, rice wine, sesame oil, and garlic in a small bowl. Brush over shrimp. Cover and chill 1 hour.

◆ To make dip, mix together rice vinegar, sugar, cilantro, and ginger in a small bowl. Cover and chill until required.

◆ Place shrimp on a grill rack and cook 1 or 2 minutes on each side, basting with marinade, until bright pink.

◆ Garnish shrimp with cilantro leaves and ginger strips and serve with ginger dip.

Squid with Eggplant and Arugula

MAKES 4 SERVINGS

2 GARLIC CLOVES, FINELY CHOPPED

2 TABLESPOONS OLIVE OIL

JUICE 1 LEMON

1 TEASPOON SWEET CHILI SAUCE

2 SMALL RED CHILIES, SEEDED AND CHOPPED

1½ POUNDS BABY SQUID, CLEANED, TUBES AND TENTACLES SEPARATED

VEGETABLE OIL FOR BRUSHING

2 MEDIUM EGGPLANT, VERY THINLY SLICED

2 CUPS ARUGULA LEAVES

LEMON WEDGES, TO SERVE

◆ In a bowl mix together garlic, olive oil, lemon juice, chili sauce, and chilies. Stir squid into marinade, cover, and leave in a cool place to marinate 2 hours.

◆ Heat a griddle on a prepared grill until smoking and brush with oil. Grill eggplant slices in batches 2 minutes on each side. Transfer to a warm oven to keep warm.

◆ Remove squid from marinade and reserve marinade. Heat griddle until searing hot and fry squid about 20 seconds on each side, then transfer to a plate.

◆ Pour marinade into a small saucepan and heat gently.

◆ Arrange eggplant slices on 4 warmed plates. Pile squid on top and spoon over a little marinade. Surround each portion with a ring of arugula leaves. Serve at once, with lemon wedges.

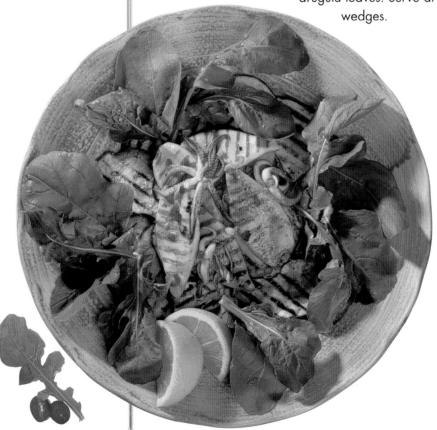

Index